CONTEMPORARY'S

EXERCISING YOUR ENGLISH

Language Skills for Developing Writers

BOOK 3

Project Editors
Betsy Rubin
Pat Fiene

CONTEMPORARY BOOKS

a division of NTC/CONTEMPORARY PUBLISHING GROUP
Lincolnwood, Illinois USA

Some of the material that appears in this book
also appears in Contemporary's *GED Writing Skills
Workbook, Book 3*. Copyright © 1988 by
Contemporary Books, Inc. (ISBN: 0-8092-5812-9)

ISBN: 0-8092-4079-3

Published by Contemporary Books,
a division of NTC/Contemporary Publishing Group, Inc.,
4255 West Touhy Avenue,
Lincolnwood (Chicago), Illinois 60712-1975 U.S.A.
© 1991 by NTC/Contemporary Publishing Group, Inc.
2 3 4 5 6 7 8 9 CCI 12 11

Editorial Director
Caren Van Slyke

Editorial
Mary Banas
Laura Larson
Bonnie Needham
Robin O'Connor

Editorial Production Manager
Norma Fioretti

Production Editor
Jean Farley Brown

Cover Design
Lois Koehler

Typography
Impressions, Inc.
Madison, Wisconsin

CONTENTS

PARAGRAPH EXERCISES

TO THE LEARNER

Contemporary's *Exercising Your English: Book 3* is designed to help you overcome common trouble spots in writing sentences, paragraphs, and essays. It focuses on sentence structure, style and diction, and organization and logic.

This workbook is one of a series of three workbooks providing extensive practice in grammar, spelling, sentence structure, and other writing skills. Your instructor may assign the workbooks in one of several ways:

1. to supplement the grammar or writing reference book you are using in class
2. to use as main texts to reinforce in-class instruction
3. to use as self-study tools for help with the specific problems that appear in your writing

Now here's a look at what you'll find in *Exercising Your English: Book 3.*

Skills Inventory

Your instructor may ask you to take the Skills Inventory test on pages 1–5 to pinpoint strengths and weaknesses in your writing skills. When you complete the Inventory, check your answers against the Answers and Explanations on pages 7–8; then refer to the Skills Inventory Evaluation Chart to see which exercises to emphasize as you work through this book.

Exercises

Before doing each exercise, read the brief writing guide at the top of the page. This guide will help you focus on the writing skill you'll need to use in the exercise. Be sure, also, to read and follow the directions carefully as you do the exercise. Then check your answers by using the Answer Key in the back of this book. If you make more than a few errors, review the writing guide, check your writing reference book or perhaps a dictionary, or see your instructor for more help.

Review Exercises

After each section is a review exercise that will help you pull together what you have just practiced. These exercises give you the chance to find out if you still need to study the writing skills covered in the section. Be sure to check your answers against the Answer Key as soon as you complete the review exercise.

Final Skills Inventory

When you have finished the workbook, you can take the Final Skills Inventory on pages 63–67 to see how well you have learned all the material you have practiced. Again, be sure to check your answers against the Answers and Explanations that follow the Inventory. If you discover you are still having problems, use the Final Skills Inventory Evaluation Chart to identify the specific areas you need to review.

A Word About Writing and Success

In recent years, many employers have noted that they have difficulty finding employees who write well. Many people in the work force do not possess the basic skills needed for writing reports, business letters, and even simple memos. People who do have good writing skills have a definite edge in the job market.

Exercising Your English: Book 3 gives you practice in the formal writing skills that are the backbone of successful academic and business writing. Your ability to write formally, clearly, and correctly will earn you respect and give you a head start for success in education and in the competitive job market. We hope you'll enjoy doing the exercises, and we wish you all the best in the future!

SKILLS INVENTORY

Part I SENTENCE STRUCTURE, STYLE, DICTION

1. The foreman glared at Jim when the assembly line stopped; <u>he</u> seemed to be having a bad day.
   - **(1)** he
   - **(2)** the man
   - **(3)** the man at work
   - **(4)** Jim
   - **(5)** somebody

2. <u>While he was adjusting the seat position in his car.</u>
   - **(1)** While he was adjusting the seat position in his car.
   - **(2)** While adjusting his car's seat position pinched his finger.
   - **(3)** While adjusting the seat position in his car, which hurt him.
   - **(4)** While he was adjusting the seat position in his car, he pinched his finger.
   - **(5)** Hurt in his car, while he was adjusting his seat position.

3. Gina lost her money in the vending <u>machine it</u> was out of order.
   - **(1)** machine it
   - **(2)** machine, it
   - **(3)** machine it,
   - **(4)** machine; it,
   - **(5)** machine; it

4. <u>Since antibiotics were discovered, bacterial</u> infections have generally become controllable.
   - **(1)** Since antibiotics were discovered, bacterial
   - **(2)** Since antibiotics were discovered. Bacterial
   - **(3)** Since antibiotics were discovered bacterial
   - **(4)** Since discovering antibiotics, bacterial
   - **(5)** Antibiotics being discovered, bacterial

5. The children's <u>shrieking led to the crash in the back seat.</u>
   - **(1)** shrieking led to the crash in the back seat.
   - **(2)** shrieking led to, in the back seat, the crash.
   - **(3)** shrieking in the back seat led to the crash.
   - **(4)** shrieking led to the crash, in the back seat.
   - **(5)** shrieking, led to the crash, in the back seat.

(continued)

2

6. The farm workers walked <u>out of the fields a meeting had been called</u> to discuss a possible strike.
    (1) out of the fields a meeting had been called
    (2) out of the fields; a meeting had been called
    (3) out of the fields, a meeting had been called
    (4) out of the fields; because a meeting had been called
    (5) out of the fields, because, a meeting had been called

6. ◯ ◯ ◯ ◯ ◯
   1 2 3 4 5

7. Because of <u>overspending, you paid your bills late, and overdrawing on your checking account,</u> you have been denied credit at this department store.
    (1) overspending, you paid your bills late, and overdrawing on your checking account,
    (2) overspending, you pay bills late, and you overdraw on your checking account,
    (3) overspending, and paying bills late, and you overdraw on your checking account,
    (4) overspending, paying bills late, and overdrawing on your checking account,
    (5) you overspend, paying bills late, and overdrawing on your checking account,

7. ◯ ◯ ◯ ◯ ◯
   1 2 3 4 5

8. <u>Because</u> Larry likes eggs, he avoids them for health reasons.
    (1) Because
    (2) Since
    (3) When
    (4) Unless
    (5) Although

8. ◯ ◯ ◯ ◯ ◯
   1 2 3 4 5

9. <u>In her electric-blue dress</u>, all of the men noticed Tina.
    (1) In her electric-blue dress
    (2) Wearing her electric-blue dress
    (3) When she wore her electric-blue dress
    (4) While wearing her electric-blue dress
    (5) Clothed in her electric-blue dress

9. ◯ ◯ ◯ ◯ ◯
   1 2 3 4 5

10. The court order dictated that the father could not <u>bug</u> his ex-wife when he picked up his children for visitation privileges.
    (1) bug
    (2) mess with
    (3) hassle
    (4) beat up on
    (5) harass

10. ◯ ◯ ◯ ◯ ◯
   1 2 3 4 5

11. I will be pleased to talk with <u>you if</u> you have any further questions.
    (1) you if
    (2) you, if
    (3) you; if
    (4) you. If
    (5) you. If,

11. ◯ ◯ ◯ ◯ ◯
   1 2 3 4 5

12. That rash appeared last year and remained for several months <u>before it clears up.</u>
    (1) before it clears up.
    (2) before it is cleared up.
    (3) before it cleared up.
    (4) before it will be cleared up.
    (5) before it will have cleared up.

12. ◯ ◯ ◯ ◯ ◯
   1 2 3 4 5

(continued)

13. We could have used the coupon that would have entitled us to one free meal, <u>and</u> it has expired.
    (1) and
    (2) or
    (3) but
    (4) however
    (5) for

13. ○ ○ ○ ○ ○
    1 2 3 4 5

14. The reason Myoung turned down dessert <u>is because he is on a diet.</u>
    (1) is because he is on a diet.
    (2) is because of a diet.
    (3) is because he is dieting.
    (4) is that Myoung is on a diet.
    (5) is that he is on a diet.

14. ○ ○ ○ ○ ○
    1 2 3 4 5

15. The wounded soldiers <u>couldn't scarcely</u> climb the hill in their weakened condition.
    (1) couldn't scarcely
    (2) could scarcely
    (3) could not scarcely;
    (4) could scarcely not
    (5) scarcely couldn't

15. ○ ○ ○ ○ ○
    1 2 3 4 5

16. Although the package felt as light as a feather, <u>it was as valuable as a gold mine.</u>
    (1) it was as valuable as a gold mine.
    (2) it was more valuable than an oil well.
    (3) its value was like that of a gold mine.
    (4) it was very valuable.
    (5) it was worth its weight in gold.

16. ○ ○ ○ ○ ○
    1 2 3 4 5

17. How long <u>was he working there</u> when he finally received a raise?
    (1) was he working there
    (2) has he been working there
    (3) did he work there
    (4) had he been working there
    (5) has he been at work there

17. ○ ○ ○ ○ ○
    1 2 3 4 5

18. The movie is filled with <u>violence; nevertheless,</u> children would be frightened by it.
    (1) violence; nevertheless,
    (2) violence, nevertheless,
    (3) violence; therefore,
    (4) violence, therefore
    (5) violence, therefore,

18. ○ ○ ○ ○ ○
    1 2 3 4 5

19. Come to the unemployment office prepared to answer many questions <u>and with your work history.</u>
    (1) and with your work history.
    (2) and your work history.
    (3) and prepared for your work history.
    (4) and, to give your work history.
    (5) and to give your work history.

19. ○ ○ ○ ○ ○
    1 2 3 4 5

20. If the truck had come any closer to the steel fence post, <u>it would have been dented.</u>
    (1) it would have been dented.
    (2) its fender would have been dented.
    (3) it would have dented it.
    (4) it would have caused a dent.
    (5) a dent would have been caused.

20. ○ ○ ○ ○ ○
    1 2 3 4 5

(continued)

4

Part II ORGANIZATION AND LOGIC

> **DIRECTIONS:** Read each of the following passages, and answer the questions below. For each question, select the best answer, and fill in the answer grid to the right.

¹Many people incorrectly think that all frogs are alike. ²In fact, there are hundreds of varieties of these amphibians. ³The many types of frogs vary not only in size and color but also in their ability to survive in and adapt to different environments. ⁴The green tree frog can change the color of its skin. ⁵From tan to green to gray to yellow. ⁶This enables the frog to hide from its enemies wherever they are encountered. ⁷Another interesting example is the poison arrow frog, which is very dangerous. ⁸This frog's skin contains a poison powerful enough to kill many larger animals that touch it. ⁹The bright red color usually scares the enemy away. ¹⁰The frog also has a red stomach. ¹¹When an enemy is near, the frog rolls on its back. ¹²In conclusion, frogs are interesting.

21. Sentence 4
    (1) should be left as it is.
    (2) should be omitted.
    (3) should begin a new paragraph.
    (4) should begin with For example,.
    (5) should begin with Therefore,.

21. ○ ○ ○ ○ ○
    1 2 3 4 5

22. What should be done with sentence 5?
    (1) It should be left as it is.
    (2) It should be omitted.
    (3) It should become part of sentence 4.
    (4) It should begin with Like,.
    (5) It should begin with It changes the color of its skin.

22. ○ ○ ○ ○ ○
    1 2 3 4 5

23. What should be done with sentence 9?
    (1) It should be left as it is.
    (2) It should be omitted.
    (3) It should be placed after sentence 10.
    (4) It should be placed after sentence 11.
    (5) It should begin a new paragraph.

23. ○ ○ ○ ○ ○
    1 2 3 4 5

24. What should be done with sentence 12?
    (1) It should be left as it is.
    (2) It should be changed to These two examples illustrate how different frogs can be.
    (3) It should be changed to However, these frogs have much in common.
    (4) It should begin with Finally, not In conclusion.
    (5) The entire sentence should be joined to Sentence 11 with a semicolon.

24. ○ ○ ○ ○ ○
    1 2 3 4 5

25. If the passage were to be divided into two paragraphs, the second paragraph should begin with
    (1) sentence 3.
    (2) sentence 4.
    (3) sentence 7.
    (4) sentence 10.
    (5) sentence 12.

25. ○ ○ ○ ○ ○
    1 2 3 4 5

(continued)

¹Here are some tips for washing windows in the best and most thorough manner. ²First of all, don't wash windows that are in direct sunlight, or they will streak. ³If you are washing both inside and out, rub one side horizontally and the other vertically. ⁴That way, you can tell which side has streaks, if any appear. ⁵A good cleaning solution is vinegar and water, which is inexpensive too. ⁶Newspaper works well for wiping cleaned windows dry. ⁷Newspapers have many household uses. ⁸Most importantly, wash your windows frequently because the dirt doesn't build up and make your job very difficult.

26. The sentence that best expresses the main idea of the paragraph is
   (1) sentence 1.
   (2) sentence 2.
   (3) sentence 6.
   (4) sentence 7.
   (5) sentence 8.

26. ○ ○ ○ ○ ○
   1 2 3 4 5

27. In sentence 3, both inside and out should be
   (1) left as it is.
   (2) changed to inside and out.
   (3) changed to both inside and also outside.
   (4) changed to either the inside and outside of the windows.
   (5) changed to both the inside and the outside of the windows.

27. ○ ○ ○ ○ ○
   1 2 3 4 5

28. Sentence 5 should be
   (1) left as it is.
   (2) omitted.
   (3) made into two sentences, divided after water.
   (4) changed to A good and inexpensive cleaning solution is vinegar and water.
   (5) changed to Vinegar is cheap and does a good job.

28. ○ ○ ○ ○ ○
   1 2 3 4 5

29. Sentence 7 should
   (1) be left as it is.
   (2) be omitted.
   (3) begin with the word because and combined with sentence 6.
   (4) be changed to The household uses of newspapers are infinite.
   (5) be changed to Who could imagine all the uses for newspapers?

29. ○ ○ ○ ○ ○
   1 2 3 4 5

30. In Sentence 8, because should be
   (1) left as it is.
   (2) preceded by a comma.
   (3) changed to on account of.
   (4) changed to so that.
   (5) changed to in so far that.

30. ○ ○ ○ ○ ○
   1 2 3 4 5

Answers and Explanations begin on page 7.

SKILLS INVENTORY EVALUATION CHART

> **DIRECTIONS:** After completing the Skills Inventory, check your answers by using the Skills Inventory Answers and Explanations, pages 7 and 8. Write the total number of *correct* answers for each skill area on the blank lines below. If you have *more than one incorrect* answer in any skill area, you need more practice. The chart shows you which workbook exercises you'll need to review.

Skill Area	Item Numbers	Total	Number Correct	Exercise Numbers
Part I				
Correct sentence structure	2, 3, 6	3	_____	1–12, 26
Misplaced and dangling modifiers	5, 9	2	_____	20–21, 26
Conjunctions	8, 13, 18	3	_____	2–4
Parallel structure	7, 19	2	_____	13–14, 17–18, 26
Verb tense	12, 17	2	_____	15–18, 26
Pronoun reference	1, 20	2	_____	19
Style and diction	10	1	_____	22–23, 25
Redundancy	14	1	_____	24–25, 26
Double negatives	15	1	_____	24–25
Mixed comparisons	16	1	_____	24–25
Part II				
Topic sentences	26	1	_____	27–28, 30
Unity	29	1	_____	29–30
Transitions	21, 30	2	_____	31–32, 35
Logical order	22, 23, 24	3	_____	34–35
Conciseness and clarity	27, 28	2	_____	33, 36–39
Paragraphing	25	1	_____	40–42

Note: Items 4 and 11 are correct.

Answers and Explanations SKILLS INVENTORY

> **DIRECTIONS:** After completing the Skills Inventory (pages 1–5), use the Answers and Explanations to check your work. *On these pages,* circle the number of each item you correctly answered. Then turn to the Skills Inventory Evaluation Chart (page 6), and follow the directions given.

Part I SENTENCE STRUCTURE, STYLE, DICTION

1. **(4)** Only this choice makes clear who seemed to be having a bad day—Jim. All of the other choices leave the sentence ambiguous.

2. **(4)** Only sentence (4) is a complete sentence. It contains an independent clause, which includes a subject and a predicate and expresses a complete thought.

3. **(5)** The original version is a run-on sentence. A semicolon is needed to join the two closely related sentences.

4. **(1)** The original form of the sentence correctly joins the dependent clause beginning with *since* to the rest of the sentence.

5. **(3)** The prepositional phrase *in the back seat* should be placed next to the word it describes, *shrieking.* The original version implies that the crash happened in the back seat.

6. **(2)** The original version is a run-on sentence. Choice (2) correctly joins the two sentences with a semicolon.

7. **(4)** Only version (4) has all three verbs in the series in parallel form—*overspending, paying,* and *overdrawing.*

8. **(5)** Only *Although* expresses the correct relationship between the two clauses of the sentence.

9. **(3)** The original version of the sentence implies that the men were wearing Tina's dress. Only version (3) makes it clear that Tina is wearing it.

10. **(5)** Only the word *harass* is consistent with the formal style of the sentence.

11. **(1)** The original version of the sentence is correct. No punctuation is needed before a dependent clause that follows an independent clause.

12. **(3)** The entire sentence is set in the past. Therefore, the verb *clear* should be in the past tense.

13. **(3)** The conjunction *but* best expresses the relationship between the two ideas in the compound sentence.

14. **(5)** Choices (1), (3), and (4) are redundant; that is, they unnecessarily repeat the same idea. Choice (2) changes the meaning of the sentence. Only choice (5) communicates the original meaning but without the redundancy.

15. **(2)** Only choice (2) avoids two negative words together (a double negative).

(continued)

16. **(4)** Choice (4) is the only sentence that does not make a mixed comparison.

17. **(4)** The sentence contains two actions in the past. He had started work before he received a raise. Therefore, the past perfect is used to express the first event (starting work), and the simple past is used to express the second event (receiving the raise).

18. **(3)** The relationship between the two ideas—the violence of the movie and the children's fear—is best expressed by the word *therefore*. *Therefore*, used as a conjunctive adverb, should be preceded by a semicolon and followed by a comma.

19. **(5)** This sentence contains two parts that should be in the same (parallel) form: *to answer many questions* and *to give your work history*.

20. **(2)** In the original version of the sentence, the word *it* could be referring to the truck *or* to the steel fence post. Thus, we don't know which would have been dented. This confusion is cleared up by pointing out that the fender (a part of the truck) would have been dented.

Part II ORGANIZATION AND LOGIC

21. **(4)** The transition words *For example* clearly relate the ideas of the two sentences.

22. **(3)** The description of specific ways in which this frog can change its colors is a fragment and should be in the same sentence with the statement it is illustrating.

23. **(4)** Since this sentence refers to the color of the frog's stomach, it must come after the sentences that first give the information that the stomach is red and that the red stomach is displayed when the frog is in danger.

24. **(2)** Only choice (2) correctly summarizes the information in the paragraph.

25. **(3)** This sentence could begin a paragraph describing the poison arrow frog.

26. **(1)** Sentence 1 is the topic sentence of the paragraph. All the other sentences give supporting details and facts.

27. **(5)** Choice (5) makes it clear that the window washer will not be both inside and outside but will instead be washing both sides of the window.

28. **(4)** This sentence is important to the tips listed in the passage, so it should not be omitted. However, it could be written more concisely by putting the two adjectives *good* and *inexpensive* together. Doing so would also make it clear that the cleaning solution is what is inexpensive.

29. **(2)** This sentence should be omitted. Though it may be true, it is irrelevant to the main topic of the paragraph.

30. **(4)** *So that* best expresses the relationship between the two ideas in the sentence.

Exercise 1   SIMPLE SENTENCES

A **simple sentence** consists of one independent clause. An **independent clause** has a subject and a predicate that communicate a complete thought. The subject tells who or what the clause is about. The predicate (or verb) tells what the subject does or is:

Manuel studies hard. (simple sentence; one independent clause)

He is a fine student. (simple sentence; one independent clause)

A special type of simple sentence is a **command**. The subject of a command—the word *you*—is understood rather than spoken or written:

Finish the assignment. (The subject is understood to be *you*.)

DIRECTIONS: In each of the following simple sentences, underline the subject once and the predicate twice. If a subject is understood, write it in parentheses after the sentence.

Examples: *Tania and I like detective stories.*
Open the door. (you)

1. Margarita sings in the church choir.
2. My brother and I fight constantly.
3. Go to your math class.
4. It is a good plan.
5. Are you going to the party?
6. Help me!
7. Sam has several brothers and sisters.
8. My new Porsche was dented by a stone.
9. After the game, we felt totally exhausted.
10. New Orleans is my favorite city.
11. Ms. Jenks interviewed me for the job.
12. Red beans and rice make a tasty side dish.
13. Before each class, review your notes from the previous class.
14. Tania seems excited about her promotion.
15. I became interested in basketball because of my brother.

Answers begin on page 71.

Exercise 2   COMPOUND SENTENCES I

A **compound sentence** consists of two simple sentences (independent clauses) joined by a conjunction. One way you can form a compound sentence is to join two simple sentences with a comma and a **coordinating conjunction** (*and, but, or, so, yet*):

I enjoyed talking with you, *and* I hope to see you soon.
(simple sentence)   (simple sentence)

DIRECTIONS: Join each pair of simple sentences with a comma and an appropriate coordinating conjunction.

Example: *It is supposed to rain* ___, *so* ___ *we have postponed the picnic.*

1. The engine of my car needs repair _____ the transmission is broken too.

2. It would cost a lot to have the car repaired _____ I am thinking of buying another one.

3. I would like to buy a new car _____ they are too expensive.

4. Call the used car dealer _____ find out the price range for a good used car.

5. Gonzalo tries to be on time for work _____ he is always late.

6. He rarely goes to bed on time _____ he has trouble getting up in the morning.

7. Every evening he sets his alarm clock _____ he also reminds his sister to awaken him.

8. Every morning he sleeps through the alarm _____ he ignores his sister's calls.

9. She yells, "Wake up, sleepy head _____ you will be late for work!"

10. He puts the pillow over his head _____ he goes back to sleep.

Answers begin on page 71.

Exercise 3   COMPOUND SENTENCES II

A second way to form compound sentences is to join two simple sentences (independent clauses) with a semicolon, a **conjunctive adverb**, and a comma:

She is always on a diet*; however,* she never seems to lose weight.

Below is a list of common conjunctive adverbs and their meanings:

moreover, furthermore, in addition (mean the same as *and*)

however, on the other hand (mean the same as *but* and *yet*)

otherwise (means the same as *or*)

therefore, as a result, consequently (mean the same as *so*)

DIRECTIONS: Join each pair of simple sentences with a semicolon, an appropriate conjunctive adverb, and a comma.

Example: *You must study ; otherwise, you will not pass the test.*

1. I wanted to get a more interesting job _____ I wanted to make more money.

2. Working with computers seemed like fun _____ I decided to take some computer classes.

3. The classes were difficult _____ I managed to pass them.

4. The school told me about job openings _____ it taught me how to answer questions on an interview.

5. My new job as a word processor in a law firm is challenging _____ the salary and benefits are good.

6. Sometimes you have to go back to school to learn new skills _____ you can get stuck in a dead-end job.

Answers begin on page 71.

Exercise 4   COMPLEX SENTENCES

A **complex sentence** consists of one independent clause and one or more dependent clauses. A **dependent clause** has a subject and a predicate, but it does not communicate a complete thought because of the word it begins with—a **subordinating conjunction:**

Connie left home. (independent clause)
since Connie left home (dependent clause)

Here are some common subordinating conjunctions:

after	since
although	until
because	when
before	where
if	while

Put a comma after a dependent clause when it is the first clause in a complex sentence:

Since Connie left home, nothing seems the same.

Omit the comma if the dependent clause is the second clause in a complex sentence:

Nothing seems the same *since Connie left home.*

DIRECTIONS: Underline the dependent clause in each of the following sentences. If a sentence needs a comma, add one on the blank line.

Example: <u>After we finish dinner</u> , we will go to the movies.

1. While you were at lunch _____ you received many calls.

2. I enjoy jogging _____ when the weather is nice.

3. If you have any questions _____ please call me.

4. Jana needs to buy a new coat _____ before winter comes.

5. We left the party early _____ because it was boring.

6. Although Carm likes living in the U.S. _____ he hopes to return to his native country someday.

7. Scott didn't drive a car _____ until he was thirty.

Answers begin on page 71.

Exercise 5   REVIEW OF SENTENCE TYPES

> **DIRECTIONS:** Label each of the sentences below by its type—*simple, compound,* or *complex.*

Example: *Will was not feeling well, so he left work early.*
      Compound
_____

1. In my opinion, breakfast is the best meal of the day.

   _____

2. We took care of their dog while they were on vacation.

   _____

3. The weather was beautiful, so we decided to go swimming.

   _____

4. If I save enough money, I will buy a new television set.

   _____

5. I used to like that band; however, their new CD is boring.

   _____

6. Beth called the store and complained about the bad service.

   _____

7. Will you be able to come to the meeting?

   _____

8. Please call me when you get back from lunch.

   _____

9. David Letterman's show is good, but I think Arsenio Hall's show is even better.

   _____

10. Be on time; otherwise, the bus will leave without you.

   _____

Answers begin on page 71.

14

Exercise 6   FRAGMENTS I

A **fragment** is an incomplete sentence. One common type of fragment occurs when a dependent clause is capitalized and punctuated as if it were a complete sentence:

If we win the championship.

Remember: Only *independent* clauses can stand alone as complete
sentences.

DIRECTIONS: Decide if each item is a complete sentence or a fragment. On the blank next to each item, write *S* if the item is a sentence or *F* if the item is a fragment.

Example: When I wrote a check to the gas company. ___*F*___

1. You need exact change to board the bus.   1. _____
2. Since I lost weight.   2. _____
3. Before you go to bed.   3. _____
4. Was the movie good?   4. _____
5. Pick up the papers.   5. _____
6. After Joe ate a late but big breakfast.   6. _____
7. Please write.   7. _____
8. Are steel-toed shoes required?   8. _____
9. The fee for taking the exam is $15.00.   9. _____
10. Have you finished the assignment yet?   10. _____
11. Stephen King's novels are always scary.   11. _____
12. If you want to get ahead in today's economy.   12. _____
13. The elevator had been out of order.   13. _____
14. Bran is a good source of fiber in the diet.   14. _____
15. February is the shortest month.   15. _____
16. Although the paint was peeling.   16. _____
17. It is cold.   17. _____
18. You should have a chest x-ray.   18. _____
19. When the leaves begin to fall from the trees.   19. _____
20. Leave the flowers alone.   20. _____

Answers begin on page 71.

Exercise 7   FRAGMENTS II

To correct a dependent-clause fragment, attach it to an appropriate sentence:

If you want to stay healthy. (dependent-clause fragment)
Drink plenty of water. (sentence)

If you want to stay healthy, drink plenty of water.

> **DIRECTIONS:** Find the three dependent-clause fragments in the
> following passage. Then, on the lines provided, rewrite
> the entire passage so that there are no fragments.

Although vegetables are nutritious. I have hated them ever since
I was a child. The very sight of cauliflower makes me break into
a cold sweat. Smothering it with cheese sauce doesn't help.
Because I can still taste the cauliflower. Broccoli also makes me
sick. I hate the way it smells while it is cooking. I dislike beets
even more. Steamed, boiled, baked, or broiled, they look bad
and taste worse. Spinach is the worst of all. Whenever I lay eyes
on it. I think of lawn cuttings. To me, fruits, dairy products, and
meats are delicious. But when it comes to vegetables, count me
out.

_____

_____

_____

_____

_____

_____

Answers begin on page 71.

Exercise 8   FRAGMENTS III

A second type of fragment occurs when a sentence is missing a subject or a complete predicate. To revise fragments like these, add the missing parts:

Works out in the gym. (Add the missing subject.)
Goldie works out in the gym.

One of the musicians in the band. (Add the missing predicate.)
One of the musicians in the band *sang*.

DIRECTIONS: Each item below contains a fragment and two rewritten versions. Put an *X* on the blank in front of the version that makes a complete sentence.

Example: *To do well in school.*

   X   *a. To do well in school, you must study.*

        b. To do well in school and on the job.

1. The home that we are renting.

       a. The home that we are renting and that we want to buy.

       b. The home that we are renting has a spacious yard.

2. Drooping from the plant.

       a. The petals drooping from the plant.

       b. The petals were drooping from the plant.

3. Having enjoyed Eddie Murphy's movies.

       a. My brother, having enjoyed Eddie Murphy's movies and comedy routines.

       b. My brother, having enjoyed Eddie Murphy's movies, has decided to become an actor.

4. With a nod of her head.

       a. With a nod of her head, the leader began the march.

       b. With a nod of her head and a brief command to the troops.

(continued)

5. Driving along Highway 1.

_____ **a.** Driving along Highway 1, you will follow the coast.

_____ **b.** All of the cars and vans driving along Highway 1.

6. Was smaller than I had imagined.

_____ **a.** Was smaller than I had imagined it to be.

_____ **b.** The hamburger was smaller than I had imagined.

7. Tired from a long day at work.

_____ **a.** Tired from a long day at work, Velma went to bed.

_____ **b.** Tired from a long day at work and a lack of sleep.

8. To earn the respect of other people.

_____ **a.** To earn the respect of other people and respect for oneself.

_____ **b.** To earn the respect of other people is important to me.

9. The best part of the whole movie.

_____ **a.** The best part of the whole movie being the end.

_____ **b.** The best part of the whole movie was the end.

10. Is a beautiful place to visit.

_____ **a.** It is a beautiful place to visit.

_____ **b.** Being that it is a beautiful place to visit.

11. The main problem with our bus system.

_____ **a.** The main problem with our bus system, in the opinion of one rider.

_____ **b.** The main problem with our bus system is overcrowding.

12. Having overcome her fear of heights.

_____ **a.** Ayuko, having overcome her fear of heights, felt proud.

_____ **b.** Ayuko, having overcome her fear of heights through desensitization techniques.

Answers begin on page 71.

18

Exercise 9   REVIEW OF SENTENCE FRAGMENTS

> **DIRECTIONS:** If there is a sentence fragment in the following groups, blacken the space in the answer grid under the number corresponding to it. If all the choices are complete sentences, blacken the space numbered (5).

Example:
  (1) Be on time.
  (2) What is the matter?
  (3) Maria called you last night.
  (4) Although we worked hard.

     ○ ○ ○ ● ○
      1 2 3 4 5

1. (1) Always complaining about something.
   (2) That game was exciting!
   (3) Liz has three motorcycles.
   (4) It was fun.

    1. ○ ○ ○ ○ ○
       1 2 3 4 5

2. (1) There are no vacancies in the building.
   (2) Where did I leave my books?
   (3) I now understand how to do story problems.
   (4) Janet Jackson is a good dancer.

    2. ○ ○ ○ ○ ○
       1 2 3 4 5

3. (1) Just being there was fun.
   (2) To tell you the truth.
   (3) The wind blew before the storm.
   (4) Please call me.

    3. ○ ○ ○ ○ ○
       1 2 3 4 5

4. (1) Is a good day to take a walk.
   (2) If you rest, you will feel better.
   (3) Who is there?
   (4) I prefer brown rice.

    4. ○ ○ ○ ○ ○
       1 2 3 4 5

5. (1) I enjoy rock-and-roll music.
   (2) Luckily, no one was hurt.
   (3) Ever since the fire.
   (4) Go home!

    5. ○ ○ ○ ○ ○
       1 2 3 4 5

6. (1) One of my coworkers at the store.
   (2) Having spent our bus money, we had to walk home.
   (3) The playground was crowded with children.
   (4) Wendel knows the answer.

    6. ○ ○ ○ ○ ○
       1 2 3 4 5

7. (1) It is difficult.
   (2) Did you see that new comedy?
   (3) Being that it is rude.
   (4) Here comes the mail.

    7. ○ ○ ○ ○ ○
       1 2 3 4 5

8. (1) Out of the frying pan and into the fire.
   (2) How is he?
   (3) We won!
   (4) To be a professional singer is my goal.

    8. ○ ○ ○ ○ ○
       1 2 3 4 5

Answers begin on page 71.

Exercise 10   RUN-ON SENTENCES I

When sentences are put together without proper punctuation, the resulting error is a **run-on sentence.** A run-on also results when two complete sentences are connected by a comma without a coordinating conjunction:

I read the newspaper I drank my coffee. (run-on)

I read the newspaper, I drank my coffee. (run-on)

I read the newspaper, and I drank my coffee. (correct)

DIRECTIONS: Decide whether each item below is a run-on or a complete sentence. On the blank after each item, write *C* if the item is a correct sentence or *RO* if the item is a run-on.

Example: Teresa fed the dog the cat wasn't inside.   _____*RO*_____

1. Have you read the book did you see the movie?   1. _____

2. The plane took off in the storm but turned back immediately.   2. _____

3. Let's clean up and get on the road.   3. _____

4. The rug keeps slipping, someone will fall.   4. _____

5. I can't spell the word, and I can't find it in the dictionary.   5. _____

6. Where can Shana be she was here a minute ago.   6. _____

7. The tenants are angry and are planning a rent strike.   7. _____

8. You asked for change, why do you need it?   8. _____

9. Your suit is good–looking it flatters you.   9. _____

10. Everything I enjoy is fattening that's why I am overweight.   10. _____

11. The operator rang our phone, she asked if we had called her earlier for help.   11. _____

12. I hadn't seen Marsha since sixth grade, but she looked the same as I remembered her.   12. _____

13. Brandon got a haircut you should see how short it is!   13. _____

14. The letter was torn and wet.   14. _____

15. I love scary movies, they are so much fun to watch.   15. _____

Answers begin on page 72.

Exercise 11 RUN-ON SENTENCES II

There are four ways to revise run-on sentences:

1. Separate the two sentences with a period.

    That restaurant has good food I think we should eat there.
    (run-on)
    That restaurant has good food. I think we should eat there.
    (revision)

2. Separate the two sentences with a semicolon.

    That restaurant is good; I think we should eat there.

3. Form a compound sentence.

    That restaurant is good, so I think we should eat there.
    That restaurant is good; therefore, I think we should eat there.

4. Form a complex sentence.

    Because that restaurant is good, I think we should eat there.

DIRECTIONS: For each item below, put an *X* in front of the version
that is a correct sentence.

Example: _____ *a. Ruth enjoys chop suey Ted does not.*

_____*X*_____ *b. Ruth enjoys chop suey, but Ted does not.*

_____ *c. Ruth enjoys chop suey; but Ted does not.*

1. _____ **a.** I smell smoke call the fire department.

   _____ **b.** I smell smoke, call the fire department.

   _____ **c.** I smell smoke. Call the fire department!

2. _____ **a.** Can you see, or is the man's head in the way?

   _____ **b.** Can you see, is the man's head in the way?

   _____ **c.** Can you see; or is the man's head in the way?

3. _____ **a.** Go for a long walk you'll feel better afterward.

   _____ **b.** Go for a long walk, you'll feel better afterward.

   _____ **c.** If you go for a long walk, you'll feel better afterward.

4. _____ **a.** It is chilly out, you will need a sweater.

   _____ **b.** It is chilly out you will need a sweater.

   _____ **c.** It is chilly out; therefore, you will need a sweater.

5. _____ **a.** The test is tomorrow, I hope I pass.

   _____ **b.** The test is tomorrow, and I hope I pass.

   _____ **c.** The test is tomorrow I hope I pass.

Answers begin on page 72.

Exercise 12   REVIEW OF SENTENCE STRUCTURE

> **DIRECTIONS:** From each group of items below, find the correctly punctuated and complete sentence (if there is one), and fill in the space in the answer grid under the corresponding number. If none of the sentences is correct, fill in the space numbered (5).

Example: (1) *Zebras, which live in Africa.*
(2) *Like to run on wide, flat plains.*
(3) *Zebras watch out for lions, lions are their worst enemies.*
(4) *All zebras have stripes, but no two zebras look exactly alike.*

○ ○ ○ ● ○
1 2 3 4 5

1. (1) Everyone who watches what he or she eats.
   (2) Knows the importance of a low salt intake.
   (3) You would be surprised to learn about foods containing a lot of salt.
   (4) Like cereals, dried fruits, and even canned vegetables.

   1. ○ ○ ○ ○ ○
       1 2 3 4 5

2. (1) The television show "60 Minutes" has been popular for many years.
   (2) Among the highest-rated shows each week.
   (3) The show often deals with controversial issues, it raises many questions.
   (4) Brought many important social problems to the attention of its viewers.

   2. ○ ○ ○ ○ ○
       1 2 3 4 5

3. (1) Camels with one hump live in the desert, those with two humps live in snowy places.
   (2) Can go for days without food or water.
   (3) Camels store fat inside a hump and live on this fat when there is no food to eat.
   (4) The size of the hump shows how much fat the camel has left; and a small hump means the camel must eat soon.

   3. ○ ○ ○ ○ ○
       1 2 3 4 5

4. (1) Abraham Lincoln, sixteenth president of the United States.
   (2) Was assassinated on April 14, 1865.
   (3) Attending the play *Our American Cousin* at Ford's Theater in Washington, D.C.
   (4) This was after the Civil War; and during his second term.

   4. ○ ○ ○ ○ ○
       1 2 3 4 5

(continued)

5. (1) Have you read any Sherlock Holmes stories; and do you like them?
   (2) Sir Arthur Conan Doyle is my favorite writer; I love his stories.
   (3) Especially "The Adventure of the Speckled Band."
   (4) Be sure to read Doyle's stories, I'm sure you'll become his fan too.

5. ○ ○ ○ ○ ○
   1 2 3 4 5

6. (1) The planet Saturn, with its well-known rings.
   (2) Has at least ten satellites large enough to be observed.
   (3) It is ninety-five times as large as Earth, Jupiter is the only planet larger than Saturn.
   (4) It is one of the five planets visible from the Earth with the naked eye.

6. ○ ○ ○ ○ ○
   1 2 3 4 5

7. (1) We visited Old Sturbridge Village in Massachusetts.
   (2) A working model of a nineteenth-century New England community.
   (3) Residents still milk cows by hand, they plow with tools used by colonists.
   (4) Allows us to step back in time and see history in action.

7. ○ ○ ○ ○ ○
   1 2 3 4 5

8. (1) "Sesame Street" is excellent, it deserves all the credit it gets.
   (2) Teaches viewers the alphabet and how to count.
   (3) The show is so clever that even parents can watch it without becoming bored.
   (4) Some of the most lovable characters on television, and some of the best writing.

8. ○ ○ ○ ○ ○
   1 2 3 4 5

9. (1) George Bush was elected president in 1988, he took office in 1989.
   (2) Often impersonated by comedian Dana Carvey.
   (3) His wish for America: a kinder and gentler nation.
   (4) He dislikes broccoli.

9. ○ ○ ○ ○ ○
   1 2 3 4 5

10. (1) Picnics and fireworks are popular on the Fourth of July, everyone enjoys the summer weather.
    (2) Is a special national holiday.
    (3) Celebrates America's independence from England.
    (4) And is a day most people don't have to work.

10. ○ ○ ○ ○ ○
    1 2 3 4 5

Answers begin on page 72.

Exercise 13   PARALLEL STRUCTURE I

The word *parallel*, when used to describe sentence structure, means that similar parts of a sentence have the same form. The following example illustrates errors resulting from a lack of parallel structure:

NOT PARALLEL: Eating, listening to music, and *to be* with my friends are my favorite pastimes.

PARALLEL: Eating, listening to music, and *being* with my friends are my favorite pastimes.

DIRECTIONS: For each pair of sentences below, decide which has parallel structure. Put an *X* on the blank in front of the correct sentence.

Example: __X__ *a. The tree is tall, leafy, and graceful.*

_____ *b. The tree is tall, has lots of leaves, and grace.*

1. _____ **a.** Get ready to fix supper, setting the table, and making the room neat.
   _____ **b.** Get ready to fix supper, set the table, and make the room neat.

2. _____ **a.** I enjoy reading the newspaper but not to watch the news on TV.
   _____ **b.** I enjoy reading the newspaper but not watching the news on TV.

3. _____ **a.** To make a mistake is human and is something that everyone does.
   _____ **b.** To make a mistake is human and that everyone does.

4. _____ **a.** Mark told Ms. Jones to rewind the tape and that he would fix the recorder.
   _____ **b.** Mark told Ms. Jones to rewind the tape and to give him the recorder so that he could repair it.

5. _____ **a.** Grandpa fed the baby, dressed her, and put her down to nap.
   _____ **b.** Grandpa fed the baby, putting her dress on, and napped.

6. _____ **a.** I plan to shop, to cook, and my housecleaning will be done before my cousin comes.
   _____ **b.** I plan to shop, to cook, and to clean before my cousin comes.

7. _____ **a.** He is friendly, handsome, and with talent.
   _____ **b.** He is friendly, handsome, and talented.

Answers begin on page 72.

Exercise 14 PARALLEL STRUCTURE II

DIRECTIONS: Correct each of the following sentences by using parallel
structure to rewrite the underlined parts of the sentence.

Example: *Juan is learning to speak, reading, and writing English all at once. Juan
is learning to speak, read____, and write____English all at once.*

1. What you earn, saving, and spending should be part of your budget.
   What you earn, _____, and _____should be part of your
   budget.

2. Michael loved Ruth for her looks, she had a good sense of humor, and she was
   intelligent.
   Michael loved Ruth for her looks, _____, and
   _____.

3. The keys to happiness are to relax, being content, and having faith.
   The keys to happiness are to relax, _____, and
   _____.

4. You must avoid bending, to cut, or to touch these negatives.
   You must avoid bending, _____, or _____these negatives.

5. The camera comes with three lenses, and you get a flash attachment.
   The camera comes with three lenses and _____.

6. I'm looking forward to meeting you and to get to know you better.
   I'm looking forward to meeting you and _____better.

7. To write your letters by hand is slower than typing them.
   _____ your letters by hand is slower than typing them.

8. Riding a bike and to swim are two good ways to exercise.
   Riding a bike and _____are two good ways to exercise.

9. I never heard anyone speak more beautifully or to convince people better.
   I never heard anyone speak more beautifully or _____.

Answers begin on page 72.

Exercise 15   VERB TENSES I

The *tense* of a verb sets a sentence in a time period. The basic tenses are illustrated below:

PRESENT: *I drive*   PRESENT PERFECT: *I have driven*
PAST: *I drove*   PAST PERFECT: *I had driven*
FUTURE: *I will drive*   FUTURE PERFECT: *I will have driven*

When you combine clauses and sentences, you must be certain that all of the verbs are in the proper tense. The verb in one part of the sentence will have an effect on the verbs in other parts of the sentence. The examples below illustrate proper verb tenses in clauses and sentences:

> Mr. Greenspan *smokes* a pipe while he *reads.*
> (both verbs in present tense)

> If I *smoke* while I work, I *will lose* my job.
> (first verb in present, second verb in future)

> John *had cleaned* his house before his mother *arrived.*
> (first verb in past perfect, second verb in past)

DIRECTIONS: In each sentence below, form the proper tense of the verb that appears in parentheses below each blank. Write the correct verb form on the blank.

Example: When I moved the refrigerator, I _____*felt*_____ *my*
                                      (feel)

back go out.

1. After the rain stopped, the sun _____ out.
                              (come)

2. Willie has $5.00, but he _____ $3.00 more.
                        (need)

3. Some people feel ill when they _____ a meal.
                         (skip)

4. John had gone shopping before he _____ dinner.
                       (cook)

5. As soon as you arrived, the party _____ livelier.
                     (get)

6. I suddenly realized that I _____ my wallet.
                 (forget)

7. The library was closing as we _____ .
                 (leave)

8. Gene is very busy and wishes he _____ more time
                     (have)
  for his family.

9. Heather had eaten only one piece of pizza when she

  _____ to feel full.
     (begin)

10. Ever since Nathaniel met Samantha, he _____
                            (seem)
  deliriously happy.

Answers begin on page 72.

Exercise 16 VERB TENSES II

Errors in verb tense occur when the verbs in a sentence do not express the intended time references. The examples below illustrate errors in verb tense and show how they can be corrected:

INCORRECT: When we are low on cash, we ate at McDonald's.
CORRECT: When we *are* low on cash, we *eat* at McDonald's.
(both present tense)

INCORRECT: If the car won't start, Greg is jumping the battery.
CORRECT: If the car *won't* start, Greg *will jump* the battery.
(present and future)

DIRECTIONS: If you see an error in the tense of an underlined verb, cross out the mistake, and write the correction above it. If the sentence is correct, write *OK*.

Example: *That rash looks serious and is* ~~needing~~ *needs to be checked by a doctor.*

1. When I was young, I <u>like</u> to visit my grandmother.

2. Yolanda <u>will read</u> the book before she saw the movie.

3. Ryan checked a dictionary but <u>was</u> unable to find the word.

4. We can hear the thunder, so we <u>expected</u> a storm.

5. Joe's parents had chosen only girls' names before they <u>had known</u> their baby was a boy.

6. We had walked three blocks before we <u>have missed</u> one of the children.

7. As the teacher was talking, Danny <u>is falling</u> asleep.

8. Since this morning, I <u>had felt</u> somewhat dizzy.

9. I would get married if I <u>have</u> more money.

10. If Bernie is smart, he <u>asked</u> for alimony from Sheila.

11. Time flew quickly while we <u>had played</u> the game.

12. If you are depressed, you <u>should have called</u> the hot line.

13. During yesterday's fire, the firefighters broke the windows and <u>had thrown</u> the furniture out.

14. The crowd is cheering for the senator and <u>wants</u> to show its support.

Answers begin on page 72.

Exercise 17 REVIEW OF VERBS AND PARALLELISM I

> **DIRECTIONS:** In each of the following sentences, four parts have been underlined. If one of these parts does not conform to the rules of parallel structure or verb tense, fill in the space in the answer grid under the number corresponding to it. If all of the underlined parts are correct, fill in the space numbered (5).

Example: The room was bright, <u>cheery</u> and <u>having a friendly look,</u> but it still <u>wasn't</u> <u>practical</u> for my office.

```
1 ● 3 4 5
1 2 3 4 5
```

1. When Dan was a baby, his mother <u>overfed</u> him; now he <u>is</u> <u>plump</u> and <u>who overeats</u>.

   1. ○ ○ ○ ○ ○
       1 2 3 4 5

2. The bowling trophy is <u>brass</u> and <u>needing to be polished,</u> or it <u>will become</u> <u>dull</u>.

   2. ○ ○ ○ ○ ○
       1 2 3 4 5

3. I always look in the encyclopedia when I <u>couldn't</u> find an answer, <u>need</u> information, or <u>want</u> <u>to know</u> more about a topic.

   3. ○ ○ ○ ○ ○
       1 2 3 4 5

4. If the light blinks, it <u>means</u> that the bulb <u>is getting</u> old and <u>should be replaced</u> before it <u>goes</u> out altogether.

   4. ○ ○ ○ ○ ○
       1 2 3 4 5

5. I feel chilly, my feet <u>are</u> <u>cold</u>, and my fingers <u>were</u> <u>stiff</u>.

   5. ○ ○ ○ ○ ○
       1 2 3 4 5

6. The Millers <u>have been</u> married twenty-five years, which <u>is</u> five years longer than I <u>have been married</u> before I <u>was</u> divorced.

   6. ○ ○ ○ ○ ○
       1 2 3 4 5

7. If the phone rings, you <u>should answer</u> it; be sure you <u>get</u> the caller's <u>name</u> and <u>what his or her number is</u>.

   7. ○ ○ ○ ○ ○
       1 2 3 4 5

8. I <u>forgot</u> that I <u>had already told</u> him about the incident, so I <u>was</u> embarrassed when he <u>tells</u> me he already heard about it.

   8. ○ ○ ○ ○ ○
       1 2 3 4 5

(continued)

9. Richard <u>has</u> a good build, <u>earns</u> a good living, and even
   ₁   ₂

   <u>takes</u> care of his widowed mother, but he just <u>isn't</u> my type.
   ₃   ₄

9. ○ ○ ○ ○ ○
    1 2 3 4 5

10. The puppy is frisky, <u>adorable</u>, and <u>well behaved</u>; if only
    ₁   ₂

    all dogs <u>are</u> so <u>pleasant</u>.
    ₃   ₄

10. ○ ○ ○ ○ ○
    1 2 3 4 5

11. The basement is damp, <u>musty</u>, and <u>smelling of mildew</u>;
    ₁   ₂

    even a good cleaning <u>will not</u> make it <u>livable</u>.
    ₃   ₄

11. ○ ○ ○ ○ ○
    1 2 3 4 5

12. On this program you will see exercises, <u>recipes</u>,
    ₁

    <u>household hints</u>, and <u>you hear</u> <u>music</u> as well.
    ₂   ₃   ₄

12. ○ ○ ○ ○ ○
    1 2 3 4 5

13. If the storm continues, we <u>will need</u> food and <u>firewood</u>;
    ₁   ₂

    furthermore, we <u>are having</u> <u>to drink</u> bottled water.
    ₃   ₄

13. ○ ○ ○ ○ ○
    1 2 3 4 5

14. What do you want most: <u>fame</u>, <u>fortune</u>, <u>health</u>, or
    ₁   ₂   ₃

    <u>to have someone love you</u>?
    ₄

14. ○ ○ ○ ○ ○
    1 2 3 4 5

15. If I had seen the uniform before I <u>was interviewed</u>, I
    ₁

    wouldn't <u>had taken</u> this job! I'd rather <u>quit</u> than <u>wear</u> it.
    ₂   ₃   ₄

15. ○ ○ ○ ○ ○
    1 2 3 4 5

16. Were you scared when you <u>saw</u> the light flashing and
    ₁

    <u>heard</u> the <u>horns</u> <u>to sound</u> their warning?
    ₂   ₃   ₄

16. ○ ○ ○ ○ ○
    1 2 3 4 5

17. When I have free time, I <u>enjoy</u> <u>bowling</u>, <u>jogging</u>, and
    ₁   ₂   ₃

    <u>when I can swim</u>.
    ₄

17. ○ ○ ○ ○ ○
    1 2 3 4 5

18. If the mail comes while I <u>was</u> gone, please <u>tell</u> the letter
    ₁   ₂

    carrier <u>to stop</u> delivering the mail until I <u>notify</u> her.
    ₃   ₄

18. ○ ○ ○ ○ ○
    1 2 3 4 5

19. Marissa <u>will keep</u> her maiden name after she is married;
    ₁

    she <u>doesn't</u> want <u>to lose</u> her identity after she <u>became</u>
    ₂   ₃   ₄

    Dan's wife.

19. ○ ○ ○ ○ ○
    1 2 3 4 5

20. The children read all their books, <u>played</u> all their <u>games</u>,
    ₁   ₂

    and <u>had done</u> all their <u>puzzles</u>.
    ₃   ₄

20. ○ ○ ○ ○ ○
    1 2 3 4 5

Answers begin on page 72.

Exercise 18   REVIEW OF VERBS AND PARALLELISM II

> **DIRECTIONS:** Beneath each sentence are five ways of writing the underlined part. Answer (1) is always the same as the part that is underlined. Choose the answer that makes the best sentence, and fill in the space in the answer grid under the number corresponding to it.

Example: *When I left the store, I will carry three packages.*
      (1) will carry
      (2) had carried
      (3) carry
      (4) carried
      (5) have carried

        ○ ○ ○ ● ○
        1 2 3 4 5

1. People like Christy for her personality, her kindness, and <u>since she is honest</u>.
   - (1) since she is honest
   - (2) her honesty
   - (3) that she is honest
   - (4) being honest
   - (5) the fact that she is honest

   1. ○ ○ ○ ○ ○
       1 2 3 4 5

2. The plant will die if it <u>didn't have</u> enough water.
   - (1) didn't have
   - (2) wouldn't have
   - (3) will not have
   - (4) doesn't have
   - (5) isn't having

   2. ○ ○ ○ ○ ○
       1 2 3 4 5

3. Education is the key to success, to advancement, and <u>to enrichment</u>.
   - (1) to enrichment
   - (2) to how you can enrich yourself
   - (3) enriching yourself
   - (4) the way to enrichment
   - (5) enriching

   3. ○ ○ ○ ○ ○
       1 2 3 4 5

4. If John F. Kennedy <u>hasn't been assassinated</u>, our history would have been quite different.
   - (1) hasn't been assassinated
   - (2) hasn't being assassinated
   - (3) hadn't been assassinated
   - (4) wasn't being assassinated
   - (5) wasn't assassinated

   4. ○ ○ ○ ○ ○
       1 2 3 4 5

(continued)

30

5. The apartment looks nice now, but you <u>don't see</u> it before it was redecorated.

    (1) don't see
    (2) haven't seen
    (3) won't see
    (4) should see
    (5) should have seen

5. ○ ○ ○ ○ ○
     1 2 3 4 5

6. The patient looks awful; her skin is pale, her eyes are bloodshot, and <u>a blue tinge to her lips</u>.

    (1) a blue tinge to her lips
    (2) her lips are blue
    (3) blue lips
    (4) blue-looking lips
    (5) blue-lipped

6. ○ ○ ○ ○ ○
     1 2 3 4 5

7. In school we study typing and <u>how to keep books</u>.

    (1) how to keep books
    (2) the way to keep books
    (3) how you keep books
    (4) bookkeeping
    (5) teaching how to do bookkeeping

7. ○ ○ ○ ○ ○
     1 2 3 4 5

8. We couldn't pay our rent, so we <u>borrowed</u> some money.

    (1) borrowed
    (2) had borrowed
    (3) would have borrowed
    (4) borrow
    (5) will have borrowed

8. ○ ○ ○ ○ ○
     1 2 3 4 5

9. A stroke can leave you paralyzed, but many people <u>recovered</u> their ability to move.

    (1) recovered
    (2) had recovered
    (3) recover
    (4) were recovering
    (5) would recover

9. ○ ○ ○ ○ ○
     1 2 3 4 5

10. Ed checked the power lines and <u>if the plug was okay</u>.

    (1) if the plug was okay
    (2) if the plug were okay
    (3) how the plug was
    (4) to see if the plug was okay
    (5) the plug

10. ○ ○ ○ ○ ○
     1 2 3 4 5

11. Take a deep breath before the test <u>is beginning</u>.

    (1) is beginning
    (2) began
    (3) will be beginning
    (4) begins
    (5) had begun

11. ○ ○ ○ ○ ○
     1 2 3 4 5

Answers begin on page 72.

Exercise 19   PRONOUN REFERENCE

In long sentences, it is often necessary to use pronouns to refer to words in other parts of the sentence. Sometimes, the meaning of the sentence is unclear because the pronouns used could refer to more than one word. The examples below illustrate problems due to unclear **pronoun reference**:

UNCLEAR: I saw Claude and Alex, whom I can't stand.

CLEAR: I saw Alex, whom I can't stand, and Claude.

DIRECTIONS: In each of the following sentences, four pronouns have been underlined. If one of these words is unclear, blacken the space in the answer grid under the number corresponding to it. If the sentence is clear as written, blacken the space numbered (5).

Example: For graduation I received a dictionary and a locket
            1

that is engraved with my name, which I really like.
  2   3   4

⭕⭕⭕●⭕
1 2 3 4 5

1. The candle and its holder fell on the glass platters, and
                    1
    they got broken; we will have to use our other ones.
    2   3   4

1. ⭕⭕⭕⭕⭕
   1 2 3 4 5

2. If anyone sees my brother and his friend, tell him to call
       1   2   3   4
    me.

2. ⭕⭕⭕⭕⭕
   1 2 3 4 5

3. We met the Smiths and their children, and they were
    1   2   3
    rude to us.
            4

3. ⭕⭕⭕⭕⭕
   1 2 3 4 5

4. Paul parked his new car in the garage, but it leaked; now
               1   2
    he will have to pay for a new paint job, which is
    3   4
    expensive.

4. ⭕⭕⭕⭕⭕
   1 2 3 4 5

5. Leopold told his boss he was sick, and she said it was
                1   2   3
    almost time for both of them to go home anyway.
                           4

5. ⭕⭕⭕⭕⭕
   1 2 3 4 5

6. Grace asked her mother if she could take their car to the
                1   2   3
    mechanic to have it fixed.
                     4

6. ⭕⭕⭕⭕⭕
   1 2 3 4 5

7. The mother, who was furious, yelled at her son, and then
                1   2
    he shouted for someone to come and help.
    3   4

7. ⭕⭕⭕⭕⭕
   1 2 3 4 5

Answers begin on page 72.

Exercise 20 MISPLACED AND DANGLING MODIFIERS I

Place **modifiers** (words that describe another word) as closely as possible to the word they describe. Otherwise, the sentence may be unclear or unintentionally humorous:

Frank tried to catch some fish *wearing rubber boots*.
(misplaced modifier)

Wearing rubber boots, Frank tried to catch some fish.
(revision)

Also be sure modifiers are not left dangling; that is, without a subject to describe:

To enter the contest, this form must be completed.
(dangling modifier)

To enter the contest, *you must* complete this form.
(revision)

DIRECTIONS: Beneath each sentence below are five versions of the underlined part or whole sentence. Answer (1) is always the same as the underlined part or sentence. Choose the answer that best completes the sentence. Fill in the number corresponding to the correct answer.

---

1. <u>Tasting and smelling peculiar, I spit out the mushrooms</u>.
   1. ◯ ◯ ◯ ◯ ◯
       1   2   3   4   5
   (1) Tasting and smelling peculiar, I spit out the mushrooms.
   (2) I tasted and smelled peculiar when I spit out the mushrooms.
   (3) The mushrooms were spit out by me, tasting and smelling peculiar.
   (4) I spit out the mushrooms, which tasted and smelled peculiar.
   (5) Due to tasting and smelling peculiar, I spit out the mushrooms.

2. The foreman complained to the worker <u>that he had made a mistake</u>.
   2. ◯ ◯ ◯ ◯ ◯
       1   2   3   4   5
   (1) that he had made a mistake.
   (2) that the worker had made a mistake.
   (3) that there was a mistake made by him.
   (4) about his mistake.
   (5) that a mistake had been made by him.

3. <u>Feeling relieved, Lee accepted his diploma</u>.
   3. ◯ ◯ ◯ ◯ ◯
       1   2   3   4   5
   (1) Feeling relieved, Lee accepted his diploma.
   (2) The diploma, feeling relieved, was accepted by Lee.
   (3) Lee accepted his diploma, which felt relieved.
   (4) The diploma accepted felt relieving to Lee.
   (5) Accepting his diploma, it felt relieved to Lee.

(continued)

33

4. The prisoner was eager to be reunited with his wife and
   <u>daughter whom he had never seen</u>.
   (1) daughter whom he had never seen.
   (2) daughter who had never been seen by him.
   (3) with the daughter he had never seen.
   (4) daughter; he had never seen her.
   (5) daughter never been seen by him.

4. ○ ○ ○ ○ ○
   1 2 3 4 5

5. Liza's <u>song in the musical, which was hilarious,</u> had
   everyone laughing.
   (1) song in the musical, which was hilarious,
   (2) hilarious song in the musical
   (3) song in the musical, hilarious,
   (4) song in the musical which were hilarious
   (5) song in the musical that were hilarious

5. ○ ○ ○ ○ ○
   1 2 3 4 5

6. After collapsing from exhaustion, <u>I couldn't get off the
   couch</u>.
   (1) I couldn't get off the couch.
   (2) the couch wouldn't let me up.
   (3) they kept me on the couch.
   (4) they made me stay on the couch.
   (5) the couch couldn't get up.

6. ○ ○ ○ ○ ○
   1 2 3 4 5

7. Julie asked Ms. Luna if <u>her keys</u> were on the table.
   (1) her keys
   (2) the keys she had put down
   (3) her own keys
   (4) the keys that were hers
   (5) Ms. Luna's keys

7. ○ ○ ○ ○ ○
   1 2 3 4 5

8. <u>Sleeping peacefully, the birds woke Enid</u>.
   (1) Sleeping peacefully, the birds woke Enid.
   (2) Sleeping peacefully, awakened by the birds, Enid.
   (3) The birds woke Enid, who had been sleeping
   peacefully.
   (4) The birds, sleeping peacefully, woke Enid.
   (5) Enid the birds woke, sleeping peacefully.

8. ○ ○ ○ ○ ○
   1 2 3 4 5

9. If the wire touches water, <u>it could electrocute you</u>.
   (1) it could electrocute you.
   (2) you could be electrocuted by it.
   (3) electrocuted you could be because of it.
   (4) the current could electrocute you.
   (5) it could cause you to be electrocuted.

9. ○ ○ ○ ○ ○
   1 2 3 4 5

10. A board came loose from the floor, <u>and it is uneven now</u>.
   (1) and it is uneven now.
   (2) and it became uneven.
   (3) and the floor is uneven now.
   (4) and it is causing unevenness.
   (5) and where it did it is uneven.

10. ○ ○ ○ ○ ○
   1 2 3 4 5

Answers begin on page 72.

Exercise 21   MISPLACED AND DANGLING MODIFIERS II

> **DIRECTIONS:** Each sentence below has a misplaced or a dangling modifier. Revise the sentence on the blank line. **Note:** Many of the sentences can be revised in more than one way.

Example: *While cutting the flowers, a bee stung me.*

While cutting the flowers, I was stung by a bee.

1. Watching the rain, time got away from me.

_____

2. The snacks are for the guests, which are on the kitchen counter.

_____

3. Whistling and singing, the road was filled with campers.

_____

4. The baby cried for his mother, who needed a dry diaper.

_____

5. Barb's husband walked the dog, who had worked until 8 P.M.

_____

6. The salesman showed a watch to the customer that kept perfect time.

_____

7. The lost child was comforted by the police officer, who had tears in her tiny eyes.

_____

8. When steaming hot, I enjoy herb tea with lemon.

_____

Answers begin on page 73.

Exercise 22   STYLE AND DICTION I

In the study of writing, **style** refers to the way in which something is said; **diction** refers to word choice. The same message may be conveyed in different styles. While the meaning will be the same, the effect will be somewhat different:

My heart is beating fast, man.

Alas! My heart flutters.

I am experiencing heart palpitations.

The three sentences would be correct in different situations. The first is quite informal and chatty, the second is poetic, and the third sounds scientific and matter of fact. Each conveys the same message in a different style.

Style in writing should be appropriate for the situation and consistent throughout.

> **DIRECTIONS:** In each of the following sentences, underline the words that are in keeping with the style of the sentence.

Example: The minister spoke eloquently at the funeral for the (old geezer, <u>deceased gentleman</u>).

1. Tomorrow's forecast calls for a high-pressure system, high clouds, and (unbearable, hot-as-an-oven) temperatures.

2. The new manager's decisive action demonstrated that she was (not a wimp, assertive and confident).

3. I'm wasted from lugging things up and down from the alley to our new (place, abode).

4. Three suspicious-looking (dudes, males) were observed loitering in the hallway.

5. (On familial excursions, On family outings), the kids play for hours, while their parents relax.

6. My buddy from the army is the (most amusing gentleman, funniest guy) I know.

7. On the cover of *Vogue* magazine is the highest paid (babe, model) in the industry.

8. Jimi, the other kids won't play with you if you're such (a tattletale, an informer).

9. Eve is the most likely candidate for the promotion because she writes (the most effectively, like a real pro).

10. The judge warned the opposing attorneys not to (hassle, argue) in the courtroom.

Answers begin on page 73.

Exercise 23   STYLE AND DICTION II

Your diction, or choice of words, can reveal your attitude toward a person, place, or thing. For example, if you like someone who is very careful with his or her money, you might describe the person as *thrifty*. If you dislike the person, you might describe him or her as *tight-fisted*. Notice how the italicized words below communicate different attitudes, even though their definitions are the same.

Lucy is *slim and trim* since she lost weight.
Lucy is *thinner* since she lost weight.
Lucy is *skinny* since she lost weight.

Be sure that the words you use convey your intended meaning and attitude.

> **DIRECTIONS:** Underline the word that best fits the style of each
> sentence below. To help you make the best choice, you
> have been given a hint about the writer's attitude.

Example: *Writer's attitude: diplomatic*
When the firm's president (was given the boot, <u>was let</u>
<u>go</u>), the chairman of the board praised him insincerely.

1. Writer's attitude: *complimentary*
   Joni is so (petite, dwarflike) that she wears a size 5 dress.

2. Writer's attitude: *romantic*
   From month to month, the pregnant young woman
   (bloomed, ballooned) in size.

3. Writer's attitude: *critical*
   I'll never go to that (surgeon, butcher) again.

4. Writer's attitude: *annoyed*
   Whenever my younger sister had the chance, she (pawed
   over, repeatedly handled) my record collection.

5. Writer's attitude: *sarcastic*
   Yeah, I'm in the sporting goods (racket, trade).

6. Writer's attitude: *critical*
   Residents of the city-run housing project reported several
   incidents of police (brutality, mistreatment).

7. Writer's attitude: *sympathetic*
   There were many (alcoholics, drunks) at the free
   Thanksgiving Day dinner.

Answers begin on page 73.

Exercise 24   REDUNDANCY, NEGATIVES, AND COMPARISONS

Avoid **redundancy** (unnecessary repetition) of words or ideas in your writing:
REDUNDANT: Her *unusual* request was *out of the ordinary*.
CORRECTED: Her request was unusual.
      OR: Her request was out of the ordinary.

Avoid **double negatives** in your writing:
WRONG: The store *won't* take *nothing* but cash.
RIGHT: The store won't take anything but cash.
  OR: The store will take nothing but cash.

Avoid **mixed comparisons:**
MIXED
COMPARISON: As light *as a cloud*, the horse pranced *like a ballerina*.
          (The horse is compared to both a cloud and a dancer.)
IMPROVED: Light on its feet, the horse pranced like a ballerina.

DIRECTIONS: Each sentence below contains one of the problems described above. Revise each sentence on the blank beneath it. **Note:** Sentences can be revised in more than one way.

Example: *I don't want to take none of those with me.*
I don't want to take any of those with me.

1. The reason I was late was because the bus broke down.

2. Like glowing embers, her black eyes, like those of a cat, sparkled with gold.

3. The office was a hive of activity, with all the workers scurrying around like mice.

4. In these modern times, present-day Americans need to believe in the rights and responsibilities of citizenship.

5. I don't have no money for tickets.

6. The international students, who are from other countries, need help filling out their papers.

Answers begin on page 73

Exercise 25   REVIEW OF STYLE AND USE OF WORDS

> **DIRECTIONS:** Beneath each sentence below are five ways of writing the underlined part. Answer 1 is always the same as the underlined part. Circle the answer whose style and word choice best completes the sentence.

1. Have you noticed that Marion <u>doesn't have no</u> money?
   - (1) doesn't have no
   - (2) doesn't scarcely have no
   - (3) doesn't have none at all
   - (4) doesn't have any
   - (5) has hardly no

2. Doctors guarantee that this new diet will make you <u>a bag of bones</u> in three weeks.
   - (1) a bag of bones
   - (2) thinner
   - (3) a shadow of your former self
   - (4) a skeleton
   - (5) a scarecrow

3. The bride and groom looked <u>starry-eyed</u>.
   - (1) starry-eyed
   - (2) glassy-eyed
   - (3) star-crossed
   - (4) cross-eyed
   - (5) bug-eyed

4. Sometimes the day is as beautiful as a freshly bloomed rose, and other times it feels like <u>a rotten apple</u>.
   - (1) a rotten apple
   - (2) a handful of thorns
   - (3) a bad egg
   - (4) a knock on the head
   - (5) a pain in the neck

5. <u>The towering tree, which is very tall,</u> needs trimming.
   - (1) The towering tree, which is very tall,
   - (2) The huge tree, which is very tall,
   - (3) The tall, towering tree
   - (4) The tall tree
   - (5) The high, tall tree

6. Queen Elizabeth wore a <u>flashy red</u> gown.
   - (1) flashy red
   - (2) bright red
   - (3) screeching red
   - (4) glaring red
   - (5) red-hot

7. This <u>unique, once-in-a-lifetime</u> opportunity is not to be missed.
   - (1) unique, once-in-a-lifetime
   - (2) unique and, indeed, special
   - (3) one-of-a-kind and truly unique
   - (4) unusual, once-in-a-lifetime
   - (5) once-in-a-lifetime

8. The <u>fragrance</u> of the garbage was obnoxious.
   - (1) fragrance
   - (2) aroma
   - (3) odor
   - (4) scent
   - (5) sniff

Answers begin on page 73.

Exercise 26   REVIEW OF SENTENCES, STYLE, WORDS

> **DIRECTIONS:** Beneath each sentence below are five ways of writing the underlined part. Answer 1 is always the same as the underlined part. Choose the answer that has correct sentence structure, style, and diction. Fill in the number in the answer grid that corresponds to the number of the correct answer.

1. The office runs <u>efficiently. Due to everyone's cooperation.</u>
   - **(1)** efficiently. Due to everyone's cooperation.
   - **(2)** efficiently; due to everyone's cooperation.
   - **(3)** efficiently due to everyone's cooperation.
   - **(4)** efficiently; due, to everyone's cooperation.
   - **(5)** efficiently and due to everyone's cooperation.

   1. ○ ○ ○ ○ ○
       1 2 3 4 5

2. These drinks all contain the artificial sweetener <u>aspartame. Some people say it is</u> bad for your health.
   - **(1)** aspartame. Some people say it is
   - **(2)** aspartame. Some people say it is a chemical that is
   - **(3)** aspartame. Some people say it (aspartame) is
   - **(4)** aspartame, which they say is
   - **(5)** aspartame, saying it is

   2. ○ ○ ○ ○ ○
       1 2 3 4 5

3. My brother <u>is curious, with a sense of humor, and thoughtfulness.</u>
   - **(1)** is curious, with a sense of humor, and thoughtfulness
   - **(2)** is curious, humorous, and thoughtful
   - **(3)** has curiousity, with a sense of humor, and thoughtful
   - **(4)** has curiosity, humor, and is thoughtful
   - **(5)** behaves curiously, humorously, and thoughtfulness

   3. ○ ○ ○ ○ ○
       1 2 3 4 5

4. On this diet, you can eat <u>desserts; moreover, you can drink soda pop.</u>
   - **(1)** desserts; moreover, you can drink soda pop.
   - **(2)** desserts moreover you can drink soda pop.
   - **(3)** desserts, moreover you can drink soda pop.
   - **(4)** desserts. Moreover you can drink soda pop.
   - **(5)** desserts, moreover, you can drink soda pop.

   4. ○ ○ ○ ○ ○
       1 2 3 4 5

5. While the planes <u>are taking off you</u> cannot hear anyone talking.
   - **(1)** are taking off you
   - **(2)** are taking off. You
   - **(3)** are taking off; you
   - **(4)** are taking off no one
   - **(5)** are taking off, you

   5. ○ ○ ○ ○ ○
       1 2 3 4 5

(continued)

40

6. Parking near the driveway <u>and if you block the crosswalk</u> are illegal.   **6.** ○ ○ ○ ○ ○
                                                               1 2 3 4 5
   - (1) and if you block the crosswalk
   - (2) and when you block the crosswalk
   - (3) and if you leave your car near the crosswalk
   - (4) and blocking the crosswalk
   - (5) if the crosswalk is blocked

7. A nurse works <u>hard and who scarcely gets any recognition</u>.   **7.** ○ ○ ○ ○ ○
                                                               1 2 3 4 5
   - (1) hard and who scarcely gets any recognition
   - (2) hard and scarcely gets any recognition
   - (3) hard. And who scarcely gets any recognition
   - (4) hard and scarcely getting any recognition
   - (5) hard and scarcely gets no recognition

8. Sharon <u>drives</u> for hours before she ran out of gas.   **8.** ○ ○ ○ ○ ○
                                                               1 2 3 4 5
   - (1) drives
   - (2) will drive
   - (3) driving
   - (4) had driven
   - (5) will have driven

9. <u>Feeling foolish, the answer</u> was right in the dictionary.   **9.** ○ ○ ○ ○ ○
                                                               1 2 3 4 5
   - (1) Feeling foolish, the answer
   - (2) Feeling foolish there the answer
   - (3) I felt foolish because the answer
   - (4) The answer, feeling foolish
   - (5) The answer, which made me feel foolish,

10. I put the money in my wallet, but now <u>it</u> is missing.   **10.** ○ ○ ○ ○ ○
                                                               1 2 3 4 5
   - (1) it
   - (2) I find it
   - (3) I can see that it
   - (4) the money
   - (5) the lost item

11. The doctor told Michael to get bed rest, elevate his feet, and <u>pop some pills</u>.   **11.** ○ ○ ○ ○ ○
                                                               1 2 3 4 5
   - (1) pop some pills
   - (2) take some medication
   - (3) dope himself up
   - (4) swallow some stuff
   - (5) ingest some special substances

12. <u>The eagerly awaited, long-looked-forward-to day</u> had finally arrived.   **12.** ○ ○ ○ ○ ○
                                                               1 2 3 4 5
   - (1) The eagerly awaited, long-looked-forward-to day
   - (2) The day, eagerly awaited and long looked forward to,
   - (3) The eagerly awaited day
   - (4) The day so awaited and so looked forward to
   - (5) The day

Answers begin on page 73.

Exercise 27   TOPIC SENTENCES I

A *paragraph* is a group of sentences that go together because they all explain the same idea. For most paragraphs, this idea is summarized in a *topic sentence*. Often, the topic sentence is at the beginning of a paragraph, but it can also be at the end or in the middle. Whether a topic sentence is at the beginning, middle, or end of a paragraph, its purpose is always the same: to tell, in brief, the main idea of the paragraph.

DIRECTIONS: The five sentences in each item below could form a paragraph, although the sentences are not necessarily in good paragraph order. Decide which sentence should serve as the topic sentence, and circle the letter of that sentence.

Example: **(a)** *He wrote over 1,000 folk songs.*

(b) *One favorite is "This Land Is Your Land."*

(c) *His son, Arlo, has carried on his folk-singing tradition.*

(d) *Woody Guthrie had a tremendous influence on American folk music.*

(e) *Many contemporary folk artists sing Guthrie's songs.*

1. **(a)** The paint is peeling.
   (b) There are two broken windows.
   (c) Our house is in terrible shape.
   (d) We need new gutters.
   (e) Even the doorbell doesn't work.

2. **(a)** The homeless population seems to be rising.
   (b) Every day, the newspaper brings more bad news.
   (c) Drugs are ruining the lives of many young people.
   (d) Crime is again on the upswing.
   (e) Senior citizens are having more and more difficulty making ends meet.

3. **(a)** The barbecued ribs were meaty and zesty.
   (b) The coleslaw was creamy.
   (c) There was a hollow watermelon filled with fruit.
   (d) The corn on the cob was buttery and fresh.
   (e) Everything at the company picnic was delicious.

4. **(a)** More women are working than ever before.
   (b) Infants are being put into day care.
   (c) Couples are having children later in life.
   (d) The structure of the American family has changed.
   (e) There has been an increase in single-parent families.

Answers begin on page 73.

Exercise 28   TOPIC SENTENCES II

Because a topic sentence summarizes the main idea of a paragraph, it is the most general statement in the paragraph. The rest of a paragraph consists of statements that are more specific than the topic sentence. These sentences give details that explain, support, or prove the topic sentence.

DIRECTIONS: Below each paragraph are four possible topic sentences. Decide which of the sentences would make the best topic sentence for the paragraph, and circle the letter beside it.

---

1. The capital city of Botswana is Gaborone. The languages spoken in the country are English, Tswana, and Khoisan. Both Christianity and tribal religions are practiced. The economy is based mostly on raising cattle and on growing and exporting corn and peanuts. Asbestos and manganese are other important products of Botswana.
   (a) Botswana is an inland republic in southern Africa.
   (b) Botswana's economy grew in the 1970s due to the production of diamonds, copper, and beef.
   (c) In general, Botswana's climate is subtropical.
   (d) Botswana's land is mostly plateau.

2. First, I studied to be a carpenter. The housing industry slowed down, and I was laid off. Then, I tried being a salesperson. The company that hired me went bankrupt. Now, I'd like to be a cab driver, but I can't afford my own cab or the cost of gasoline.
   (a) For me, jobs are easy to come by.
   (b) I like several jobs that I have held.
   (c) I can't seem to choose a job with a secure future.
   (d) I used to want to be a computer operator.

3. They are responsible for our most precious possessions: our children. They not only care for the children's physical needs but also provide activities and intellectual stimulation. They work hard all day with few, if any, breaks and undoubtedly go home exhausted. Their work is too important and too demanding to be so poorly compensated.
   (a) I hope to be a child-care worker one day.
   (b) There is a lot of turnover among child-care workers.
   (c) Child-care workers take good care of our children.
   (d) Child-care workers deserve higher pay.

Answers begin on page 73.

Exercise 29   UNITY

Effective paragraphs are **unified.** All the sentences go together because all of them are about the same idea. To unify your paragraphs, leave out sentences that do not belong; that is, sentences that do not explain, support, or prove the main idea.

> **DIRECTIONS:** In each of the paragraphs below, there may be a sentence that doesn't belong. If there is, fill in the space in the answer grid corresponding to it. If all of the sentences belong, fill in the space numbered (5).

Example: *¹Most people know that coffee contains caffeine. ²Few people realize that tea also contains a good deal of caffeine. ³Many soft drinks contain caffeine as well. ⁴Diet soft drinks contain fewer calories than regular soft drinks.*

O O O ● O
1 2 3 4 5

1. ¹Dolores must learn to be more assertive in her job. ²She always lets people tell her what to do. ³She earns a decent salary. ⁴For this reason, she has earned the nickname "Dolores the Doormat."

1. O O O O O
1 2 3 4 5

2. ¹Chicago's weather is unpredictable. ²Within a week, temperatures may vary by as much as forty degrees. ³Sometimes, the wind will shift and the temperature will drop twenty degrees in an hour. ⁴People always say that if you don't like Chicago's weather, wait a day and it will change.

2. O O O O O
1 2 3 4 5

3. ¹All young children should be vaccinated against whooping cough. ²Another name for the disease is pertussis. ³The disease is bacterial in nature, causing a peculiar-sounding cough. ⁴You should avoid coughing on other people.

3. O O O O O
1 2 3 4 5

4. ¹Jack and Sarah enjoy all types of music. ²No matter whether it is jazz, rock-and-roll, or classical music, they never miss a concert. ³Most people don't understand the influence that the blues has had on rock-and-roll. ⁴Someday, they hope to go to the Newport Jazz Festival for a week.

4. O O O O O
1 2 3 4 5

5. ¹A growing number of young women hope to become professional athletes. ²Some train for years to get their big break in the Olympics, while others join college teams or play in career-level sports such as golf or tennis. ³Because there are now more women athletes than there were in the past, it has been predicted that the salary and respect given to women athletes will increase in the years to come. ⁴Chris Evert played tennis professionally for years.

5. O O O O O
1 2 3 4 5

(continued)

44

6. [1]Zena practices a health-conscious philosophy. [2]Her husband refuses to eat fresh fruits or vegetables. [3]Zena exercises regularly and tries to get eight hours of sleep every night. [4]She avoids unnecessary medication and foods containing additives and preservatives that she considers to be unhealthy.

6. ○ ○ ○ ○ ○
    1 2 3 4 5

7. [1]Bighorn sheep live in the mountains from western Canada to Mexico. [2]The sheep successfully survive some of nature's harshest tests. [3]They are not afraid of wolves, mountain lions, steep cliffs, bitter cold, or lack of food. [4]Lambs are often associated with Easter time.

7. ○ ○ ○ ○ ○
    1 2 3 4 5

8. [1]The children are playing quietly while I work. [2]Raising children can be a full-time occupation. [3]Children need both physical care and emotional guidance. [4]To do the job well, parents need both time and energy.

8. ○ ○ ○ ○ ○
    1 2 3 4 5

9. [1]My sister's law firm is very choosy about whom it hires. [2]To be a secretary at this firm, a person must have at least five years' legal secretarial experience. [3]He or she must also be familiar with several different kinds of computer software. [4]In addition, the person must pass stringent math, English, and shorthand tests.

9. ○ ○ ○ ○ ○
    1 2 3 4 5

10. [1]Why is fall my favorite time of year? [2]I love it, even though I know that it depresses many people who can't bear to think of winter's approach. [3]Swimming, biking, and tennis are my favorite summer sports. [4]There's nothing that I enjoy more than a walk beneath the changing leaves and a hot cup of soup to warm my chilled bones.

10. ○ ○ ○ ○ ○
    1 2 3 4 5

Answers begin on page 73.

Exercise 30   REVIEW OF TOPIC SENTENCES AND UNITY

> **DIRECTIONS:** In each item below, the numbered sentences should form a unified paragraph with a clear topic sentence. Determine which sentence is the topic sentence for the paragraph. Put the number of the topic sentence on the blank to the left of the paragraph. Determine which sentences, if any, do not belong in the paragraph. On the blank to the right of the paragraph, put the number or numbers of the sentences that do not belong.

Example   _3_   ¹*Alycia had asthma as a child.* ²*Even now, she has severe allergies.* ³*Alycia has always been a sickly person.* ⁴*She has always been beautiful.* ⁵*Now she has developed arthritis.* ⁶*Even her voice is beautiful.*   _4, 6_

1. _____ ¹Although Cleveland, Ohio, is often the target of comedy routines, it is actually a city with many attractions. ²The Cleveland Symphony Orchestra is one of the best in the world. ³If you enjoy sports, Cleveland has several professional sports teams. ⁴Music and sports are an important part of city life in the U.S. ⁵Cleveland also has several good colleges in its metropolitan area. _____

2. _____ ¹The Great Ape House is spectacular. ²The seal pool is beautiful. ³The outdoor areas for lions and tigers are most impressive. ⁴Best of all, admission is always free. ⁵Many people think that the Lincoln Park Zoo is the best zoo in a major U.S. city. _____

3. _____ ¹Our family is hooked on TV soap operas. ²At lunchtime, we never miss an episode of "All My Children." ³Early afternoon, we are glued to "General Hospital." ⁴Once I waited to go to the hospital when I was watching "Dallas." ⁵TV watching is cheaper than going out for an evening. ⁶We even watch reruns of the evening soap operas. _____

4. _____ ¹Reye's syndrome is a serious disease that strikes children, particularly those over the age of six. ²This disease affects the brain and liver and appears to be associated with such viral illnesses as chicken pox and the flu. ³The use of aspirin during these illnesses is believed to increase the risk of Reye's syndrome, so doctors no longer recommend aspirin for children. ⁴On "All My Children," Erica's daughter, Bianca, once got Reye's syndrome. ⁵It was such a relief when she recovered. ⁶Fortunately, this disease is relatively rare. _____

(continued)

5. _____ [1]Most of the arts award their outstanding participants with some type of award. [2]The Oscar is well known as the top honor in the film industry. [3]In sports, too, there are awards. [4]The Grammy is the award for a recording artist or group. [5]Perhaps less well known, but highly prized by members of the live theater community, is the Tony award. [6]The Davis Cup in tennis is an example of a sports award. [7]And the Obie is awarded to outstanding off-Broadway plays. _____

6. _____ [1]What an interesting career Diana Ross has had! [2]She began her career in the 1960s as lead singer for the Supremes. [3]After making many successful records with this group, Miss Ross left the Supremes to record on her own. [4]Many people say that she is good friends with entertainer Michael Jackson. [5]Miss Ross has also starred in movies. [6]For example, she had leading roles in _Lady Sings the Blues_ and _The Wiz_. [7]I own recordings of the sound tracks from these movies. [8]More recently, Miss Ross has done successful concert tours. _____

7. _____ [1]Some theories say that it is enough just to count your calories. [2]Others claim that you must focus on sharply cutting your intake of fat. [3]There must be dozens of different theories about dieting and as many books to support those theories. [4]My personal weakness is for pie, mainly banana cream or chocolate cream, but any type will do. [5]Many of these so-called experts are not nutritionists or doctors, and their ideas are neither medically sound nor scientifically based. [6]One diet expert was fatally shot by his jealous girlfriend. _____

8. _____ [1]It began when I scalded myself making coffee. [2]It continued when I burned my toast. [3]Usually, I prefer rye toast to white. [4]Then I missed my bus. [5]The worst was when I got my fingers caught in the elevator door. [6]I now think of my birthday as my unluckiest day this year. _____

9. _____ [1]Josef really appreciates the public library. [2]There he reads current newspapers and magazines every day. [3]It's a crime to pay $3.00 for a magazine! [4]He borrows popular books, cassettes, and videotapes. [5]For example, he now is reading a copy of _The Hunt for Red October_. [6]Sometimes, Josef just uses the library as a quiet refuge from his busy job and hectic family routine. _____

Answers begin on page 73.

Exercise 31   COHERENCE AND TRANSITIONS I

Well-written paragraphs are **coherent**. Each sentence clearly and logically leads to the next sentence. One way to create coherence is to use appropriate **transition words**. These words show the logical relationship between sentences.

In the following examples, the underlined transition words show the logical relationship between the ideas they connect:

The sky is cloudy. Therefore, I think it will rain. (shows a result or effect)

The forecast calls for clearing. However, I don't have much confidence in the prediction. (shows contrast or difference)

The sun is out. Now we can have our picnic. (shows relationship of time)

DIRECTIONS: Read the sentences and the list of words that follows them. If one transition word in a group correctly expresses the relationship between the two sentences and could connect them, circle the letter corresponding to it. If none of the transition words is appropriate, circle letter *e*.

---

1. Those batteries are almost worn out. The flashlight is dim.
   (a) however
   (b) for example
   (c) therefore
   (d) in conclusion
   (e) none is appropriate

2. Set the table. Serve the salad.
   (a) then
   (b) however
   (c) such as
   (d) on the whole
   (e) none is appropriate

3. Jerry is an excellent bowler. He has won several trophies.
   (a) eventually
   (b) also
   (c) in fact
   (d) besides
   (e) none is appropriate

4. I looked in the dictionary. I couldn't locate the word.
   (a) before
   (b) however
   (c) similarly
   (d) meanwhile
   (e) none is appropriate

5. I'm allergic to most dairy products. Cats make me sneeze.
   (a) on the other hand
   (b) beyond
   (c) moreover
   (d) therefore
   (e) none is appropriate

6. A large van blocked the parking lot. I could not park in my assigned space.
   (a) moreover
   (b) for instance
   (c) currently
   (d) as a result
   (e) none is appropriate

Answers begin on page 73.

48

Exercise 32   COHERENCE AND TRANSITIONS II

> **DIRECTIONS:** In each paragraph below, important transition words have been left out. A line has been drawn where a transition word is needed. Below each line are three possible transition words. Decide which of the three transition words best explains the logical relationship, and write that word on the line.

Example: I have been working overtime lately.

_____ *Therefore* _____ , I have been tired and
(Later, Finally, Therefore)

somewhat crabby. _____ *On the other hand* _____ , I am
(Eventually, On the other hand. Before)

earning much-needed money.

Judy gives piano lessons as a hobby. _____ ,
(1. That is, In addition, Then)

her teaching allows her to earn extra money. She is able to

teach while her children nap. _____ ,
(2. Therefore, Finally, Likewise)

she does not need to employ a baby-sitter. _____ ,
(3. As a result, Eventually, Again)

when her children are grown, she will try to become a full-time

music teacher.

We are having a big family reunion this summer.

_____ , my grandparents are
(4. Later, However, First)

coming from Arizona. _____ my
(5. Finally, At the same time, Thus)

sister-in-law and her children are coming from Colorado. We'll

all spend three days together. _____ ,
(6. Then, As a result, Before)

my brother will join us for two more days. _____ ,
(7. Consequently, For example, Finally)

my aunt will fly in from San Antonio for a big dinner celebration

with everyone.

Disabled people who wish to get around the city may

encounter many obstacles. _____ ,
(8. For example, In addition, As a result)

many street corners lack ramps. _____ ,
(9. In fact, Moreover, However)

many streets and sidewalks have bumps and cracks.

_____ , disabled people may be
(10. However, Consequently, For example)

unable to travel even a few blocks alone.

Answers begin on page 74.

Exercise 33   COHERENCE AND REPETITION

Repeating important elements is another way to show how sentences logically relate to each other. There are three main ways to create coherence through repetition:

1. Repeating key words:

    The average *price* of a *gold* necklace may change rapidly. *Gold prices* seldom stay the same for very long.

2. Using pronouns to refer to previously stated ideas:

    The thesaurus is a good reference *book*. *It* contains synonyms for overused words and expressions.

3. Repeating sentence structure:

    In summer, the *temperature soars to* 100°. *In winter,* the *temperature can fall* to 20° below zero.

> **DIRECTIONS:** Read each group of sentences, concentrating on the underlined words. Then, on the blank line, tell which of the three methods has been used to create coherence: repeating key words, using pronouns, or repeating sentence structure.

Example: *There are several reasons that I like jeans. They are not very expensive, they look good, and I feel comfortable wearing them.*
Using pronouns

1. My diet plan is very simple. <u>For breakfast, I have bran cereal and skim milk. For lunch, I have a vegetable salad and fruit. And for dinner, I have a piece of broiled fish and a potato or rice.</u>

    _____

2. Ernest Hemingway wrote <u>books</u> about adventure and challenge. One of his best <u>novels</u> tells the <u>story</u> of an aging fisherman and his struggle to catch a particular fish.

    _____

3. My dog <u>Bart</u> is a wonderful pet. <u>He</u> can do several tricks, and <u>he</u> is so well trained that I can take <u>him</u> for a walk without <u>his</u> leash.

    _____

Answers begin on page 74.

Exercise 34   LOGICAL ORDER

In addition to having a clear topic sentence, unity, and coherence, good paragraphs are also well organized. The sequence, or order of the sentences, is clear and logical.

DIRECTIONS: In each item below, the five sentences need to be put into logical order. Number each sentence 1, 2, 3, 4, or 5 on the blank to the left to indicate its proper order in the paragraph.

---

1. _____ This does not give them a real picture of Hawaii, since Waikiki is a tourist area and is not representative of the state as a whole.

   _____ A trip to lesser-known areas would give visitors a more complete picture.

   _____ Many people equate Hawaii's Waikiki Beach with the name *Hawaii* itself.

   _____ Hawaii is one of the Hawaiian Islands.

   _____ Only then would visitors begin to see all that Hawaii has to offer.

2. _____ For example, he uses his credit cards to pay for gasoline and groceries.

   _____ Furthermore, he has credit cards at most major department stores.

   _____ Ed might find himself in financial trouble from overuse of his credit cards.

   _____ Rather than use cash, he charges everything he can.

   _____ Some department-store cards are costing him 20 percent interest.

3. _____ Lamb is a popular source of meat, offering several distinct cuts.

   _____ Below the lamb chops are rib chops and loin chops.

   _____ Lamb chops are obtained from the shoulder of the animal.

   _____ Beneath the chops is the area from which leg of lamb is cut.

   _____ The final cut, the lamb shank, is useful in making soups and stews.

4. _____ She no longer wears dark-colored clothing.

   _____ Since she lost weight, Carole has changed her image.

   _____ In addition to wearing brighter clothes, she has lightened her hair color.

   _____ From mousy brown, she has progressed to flaming red.

   _____ In fact, she now wears hot pink and bright orange.

5. _____ When fire broke out in the social club, the patrons were trapped.

   _____ Consequently, the mayor moved rapidly to close down all such clubs.

   _____ The entire club had only one exit, and flames blocked the door.

   _____ As a result, most of the patrons could not escape.

   _____ The people's deaths made the city aware of the hazardous conditions of illegal social clubs.

Answers begin on page 74.

Exercise 35 REVIEW OF SENTENCE ORDER AND COHERENCE

DIRECTIONS: Read each of the following passages before answering the questions below. For each question, select the best answer. Then fill in the corresponding space in the answer grid.

¹All of these facts and many, many more are contained in the almanac. ²The almanac is an amazing resource. ³It has a wealth of information conveniently organized into one volume. ⁴Moreover, it can tell you when John F. Kennedy was born, who won the last World Series, or how many calories are in spaghetti.

1. Sentence 1 should
   (1) remain as it is.
   (2) follow sentence 2.
   (3) follow sentence 3.
   (4) follow sentence 4.
   (5) be omitted.

   1. ○ ○ ○ ○ ○
      1 2 3 4 5

2. The word *Moreover* in sentence 4 should
   (1) remain as it is.
   (2) be changed to *For example.*
   (3) be changed to *However.*
   (4) be changed to *In addition.*
   (5) be changed to *On the other hand.*

   2. ○ ○ ○ ○ ○
      1 2 3 4 5

¹It's 95° outside, but it feels like 195° in this factory. ²I don't think I can stand up for one more minute! ³Why don't the owners put fans in this plant? ⁴Or even better than that would be, why don't they install air-conditioning? ⁵Air-conditioning may be an added expense, but we deserve to be comfortable while we work.

3. In sentence 4, *Or even better than that would be* should be written
   (1) *Or even better than that would be.*
   (2) *But better than that.*
   (3) *And even better than that.*
   (4) *Better than that would be.*
   (5) *Better yet.*

   3. ○ ○ ○ ○ ○
      1 2 3 4 5

(continued)

4. Sentence 5 should
    (1) remain where it is.
    (2) follow sentence 2.
    (3) begin the paragraph.
    (4) follow sentence 3.
    (5) be omitted.

4. ○ ○ ○ ○ ○
    1 2 3 4 5

¹I plan to take the GED next month. ²Passing the test will be a major step in my life. ³My teacher has emphasized that I should not rush through the material I am studying now. ⁴Therefore, I do have a test deadline to meet. ⁵You see, I want to pass the test then so my eighteen-year-old grandson and I can graduate at the same time. ⁶This deadline is at the end of May.

5. In sentence 4, *Therefore* should
    (1) remain as it is.
    (2) be changed to *For example*
    (3) be changed to *For this reason.*
    (4) be changed to *However.*
    (5) be changed to *What is more.*

5. ○ ○ ○ ○ ○
    1 2 3 4 5

6. Sentence 6 should
    (1) remain where it is.
    (2) follow sentence 2.
    (3) follow sentence 3.
    (4) follow sentence 4.
    (5) be omitted.

6. ○ ○ ○ ○ ○
    1 2 3 4 5

¹During the American Civil War, Clara Barton began her lifetime career of relief work. ²She became involved in the International Red Cross during a trip to Europe after the Civil War. ³Even today, the Red Cross has continued Barton's work, helping the victims of flood, war, and famine throughout the world. ⁴Upon her return to the United States, she founded the American Red Cross. ⁵Furthermore, she served as its first president.

7. In sentence 5, *Furthermore* should
    (1) remain.
    (2) be changed to *However.*
    (3) be changed to *Instead.*
    (4) be changed to *Surprisingly.*
    (5) be omitted.

7. ○ ○ ○ ○ ○
    1 2 3 4 5

8. Sentence 3 should
    (1) remain where it is.
    (2) follow sentence 1.
    (3) follow sentence 4.
    (4) follow sentence 5.
    (5) begin the paragraph.

8. ○ ○ ○ ○ ○
    1 2 3 4 5

Answers begin on page 74.

Exercise 36   CONCISE WRITING I

To write concisely, use as few words as possible. One method of concise writing is **word reduction**. As the sentences below show, the first sentence can be reduced to the second with no loss of meaning.

1. Because of her extreme arthritis, it was Mary's thought that she should get a parking permit that allows the disabled to park in special places. (*wordy*)

2. Because of her extreme arthritis, Mary thought that she should get a special parking permit for the disabled.

Another way to achieve conciseness is through **combining sentences**. The examples below show how this works.

1. Alex was studying in the library. While he was studying there, he met Renee. (*wordy*)
2. While Alex was studying in the library, he met Renee.

DIRECTIONS: Beneath each item are five ways of writing the underlined part of the sentence. Answer 1 is always the same as the underlined part. Circle the number of the answer that makes the sentence the most concise. (Notice that in some of the choices there are punctuation changes.) *Be sure that your answer does not change the meaning of the sentence.*

---

1. Put the cards in a stack. <u>When they are in a stack</u>, put a rubber band around them.

    (1) When they are in a stack
    (2) Then
    (3) When you have stacked them
    (4) Having so accomplished this
    (5) Stacking them thusly

2. <u>The fare that they charge to ride the bus</u> is 90¢.

    (1) The fare that they charge to ride the bus
    (2) The fare charged for riding the bus
    (3) The bus fare
    (4) To ride
    (5) The fare for a ride on the bus

3. We have called this meeting <u>because of the fact that we want</u> to plan a rent strike.

    (1) because of the fact that we want
    (2) due to the fact that we want
    (3) owing to our desire to
    (4) for the reason that we want
    (5) in order

4. We try to eat beans for supper once a <u>week; we eat beans for supper once a week because beans</u> are economical and contain protein.

    (1) week; we eat beans for supper once a week because beans
    (2) week; we eat this way once a week because beans
    (3) week due to the fact that beans
    (4) week; we eat beans at this rate because they
    (5) week because they

Answers begin on page 74.

Exercise 37   CONCISE WRITING II

> **DIRECTIONS:** The following passage contains five sentences. The paragraph is wordy and needs to be rewritten. Through word reduction and sentence combination, rewrite the paragraph more concisely. Your rewritten paragraph should have only four sentences but should contain the same ideas as the original. *Hint:* Cross out unneeded words in the original paragraph before you rewrite it.

[1]Ever since talk-show host Oprah Winfrey, host of "The Oprah Winfrey Show," lost nearly 70 pounds of unneeded fat, thousands of Americans right here in the United States have decided to try the plan that Oprah Winfrey used. [2]The plan they have decided to try is the liquid-formula diet plan that she used. [3]Experts now suspect and, indeed, believe, however, that liquid diets often contribute to physical or psychological problems for people on liquid diets, as a matter of fact. [4]Apparently, it seems that many of these people who are dieters develop strong, intense cravings for foods containing high percentages of fat and calories. [5]Furthermore, they become accustomed to surviving and living without real food, and they fear that once they are used to going without food, they will lose all control and go berserk when they begin to start eating again.

_____

_____

_____

_____

_____

_____

_____

_____

_____

_____

Answers begin on page 74.

Exercise 38   AMBIGUITY

In the earlier exercises on sentences, you saw that good writing should be clear and concise. Exercise 19 focused on one type of ambiguity, that of unclear pronoun reference. In addition, sentences may be unclear because key words that clarify the relationship between ideas have been left out.

> Ambiguous: Many people are being laid off, a hard problem to solve. (What's a hard problem to solve?)

> Clear: Many people are being laid off. *Finding them work* will be a hard problem to solve.

DIRECTIONS: Beneath each sentence or set of sentences, you will find four ways of writing the underlined part. Answer (1) is always the same as the underlined part. Circle the number of the answer that makes the sentence or sentences clear.

Example: *The car must need a new muffler because it is noisy.*
  (1) *because it is noisy.*
  (2) *because of its noise.*
  (3) *for its noise.*
  (4) *because the car is noisy.*

1. Lorenzo can hardly pay the rent and <u>taxes. They are so high</u>.
   (1) taxes. They are so high.
   (2) taxes, which are so high.
   (3) high taxes.
   (4) taxes, high as they are.

2. We first ate the hot dogs and then the hamburgers even though <u>they were overcooked</u>.
   (1) they were overcooked.
   (2) there were too many overcooked.
   (3) everything was overcooked.
   (4) we had overcooked them.

3. Mama always encourages her children to be curious. Sometimes the children get into trouble <u>because of her</u>.
   (1) because of her.
   (2) because of her advice.
   (3) due to it.
   (4) due to her.

(continued)

4. The students were learning to speak English, <u>but not among themselves</u>.
   (1) but not among themselves.
   (2) but not for themselves.
   (3) and didn't do it among themselves.
   (4) but they preferred to speak Spanish among themselves.

5. Robert and his children often make their own ice cream, <u>which they love</u>.
   (1) which they love.
   (2) an activity they love.
   (3) which is wonderful for them.
   (4) something they really love.

6. <u>Here's the problem:</u> too little money and too much work.
   (1) Here's the problem:
   (2) The problem is that:
   (3) Problem:
   (4) It's the problem:

7. When the girls told on the boys, <u>they got into trouble</u>.
   (1) they got into trouble.
   (2) they all got into trouble.
   (3) those children got into trouble.
   (4) the boys got into trouble.

8. Although Ms. Mallon is only 21, she teaches seventh <u>grade, such a difficult age</u>.
   (1) grade, such a difficult age.
   (2) grade, so difficult an age to be.
   (3) grade; teaching twelve-year-olds can be difficult.
   (4) grade; being that age is so difficult.

9. Many city dwellers like to get <u>away, such as the Rocky Mountains</u>.
   (1) away, such as the Rocky Mountains.
   (2) away to places such as the Rocky Mountains.
   (3) away, for example, the Rocky Mountains.
   (4) away, the Rocky Mountains, for instance.

10. Our neighbors play tapes all night <u>long; they are so noisy</u>.
    (1) long; they are so noisy.
    (2) long; those people are so noisy.
    (3) long, so noisy are they.
    (4) long, and they make so much noise.

Answers begin on page 74.

Exercise 39   REVIEW OF CONCISENESS, AMBIGUITY, AND STYLE

DIRECTIONS: Each paragraph below has underlined portions. The underlined portions are numbered. Read the paragraph, and decide if each underlined portion could be improved to be *clearer,* more *concise,* or *more consistent in style.* Fill in the space in the answer grid that corresponds to the best version of the underlined portion. Answer (1) is always the same as the underlined version.

Aspirin can be found in most families' medicine cabinets. The drug is routinely used for colds, headaches, the flu, and [1]any other maladies you can come up with. Recently, however, the use of common aspirin has been questioned [2]on account of its safety. Doctors [3]say that in their expert opinions that aspirin should not be used by pregnant women, by children with flu symptoms, or by people who have ulcers.

1. (1) any other maladies you can come up with.
   (2) various other maladies.
   (3) other hurting things.
   (4) whatever.
   (5) others.

1. ○ ○ ○ ○ ○
   1 2 3 4 5

2. (1) on account of its
   (2) about its
   (3) with respect for its
   (4) in terms of its
   (5) for its

2. ○ ○ ○ ○ ○
   1 2 3 4 5

3. (1) say that in their expert opinions
   (2) demand
   (3) say expertly that
   (4) say
   (5) say, because they're experts, that

3. ○ ○ ○ ○ ○
   1 2 3 4 5

Going out can be [4]very costly. A nice dinner may cost up to $30.00 a person. A ticket to a first-run movie may cost as much as $10.00. [5]If the services of a baby-sitter are needed, that can cost from $2.00 to $5.00 per hour, depending on the number of children. [6]It's really expensive!

4. (1) very costly
   (2) real high in price
   (3) big bucks
   (4) very high
   (5) a pain in the wallet

4. ○ ○ ○ ○ ○
   1 2 3 4 5

5. (1) If the services of a baby-sitter are needed, that
   (2) A person who baby-sits
   (3) A baby-sitter's services
   (4) One who can watch your children
   (5) Some sitting

5. ○ ○ ○ ○ ○
    1 2 3 4 5

6. (1) It's
   (2) So, it's
   (3) It's all
   (4) They're
   (5) An evening out can be

6. ○ ○ ○ ○ ○
    1 2 3 4 5

Marilyn Monroe is still well known as a famous blond sex symbol, [7]excepting for her dying in 1962. Monroe was [8]at thirty-six years old when she [9]left Hollywood for Heaven.

7. (1) excepting for her dying in 1962
   (2) although she died in 1962
   (3) but for her 1962 death
   (4) in spite of her 1962 death
   (5) except she died in 1962

7. ○ ○ ○ ○ ○
    1 2 3 4 5

8. (1) at
   (2) at about
   (3) only
   (4) right about
   (5) just at the age of

8. ○ ○ ○ ○ ○
    1 2 3 4 5

9. (1) left Hollywood for Heaven
   (2) ascended to the real stars
   (3) moved on to greener pastures
   (4) died
   (5) gave up the ghost

9. ○ ○ ○ ○ ○
    1 2 3 4 5

West Point, which is both the site of and the common name for the U.S. Military Academy, is located [10]in the upstate part of the state of New York. Since 1976, West Point has accepted both men and women. To enter West Point, [11]they must be between seventeen and twenty-two years of age.

10. (1) in the upstate part of the state of New York
    (2) in the state known as New York
    (3) in upstate New York
    (4) in the northeastern U.S. state called New York
    (5) somewhere in New York

10. ○ ○ ○ ○ ○
     1 2 3 4 5

11. (1) they
    (2) those people
    (3) it
    (4) the males and females
    (5) candidates

11. ○ ○ ○ ○ ○
     1 2 3 4 5

Answers begin on page 74.

Exercise 40 PARAGRAPHING I

Within longer pieces of writing, such as essays, sentences are grouped into paragraphs, each of which focuses on one idea. This exercise gives you practice in grouping sentences with the main idea they explain.

> **DIRECTIONS:** Below are three topic sentences numbered I, II, and III. These sentences are the topic sentences for three paragraphs. Below the three topic sentences are eleven sentences. Each of the eleven sentences could support topic sentence I, II, or III. As you read each statement, decide into which paragraph (I, II, or III) it would fit, and put the number of the topic sentence on the blank in front of it. Sentence 1 has been done as an example.

Topic Sentences:

I. *I wonder if a marriage is more successful when the partners are very much alike or when they are totally different from one another.*

II. *I know a couple who think alike on every issue.*

III. *Another husband and wife whom I know illustrate the saying "opposites attract."*

III 1. Cecilia and Lawrence are as different from one another as night and day.

_____ 2. Do people with differing personalities complement or clash with each other?

_____ 3. As outgoing and sociable as she is, he is a loner and an introvert.

_____ 4. Someone once said of Alice and John that they are like twins because they are so similar to one another.

_____ 5. They are both interested in the same sports.

_____ 6. When they vacation, he wants to camp by an isolated stream, and she wants to go where the action is.

_____ 7. What keeps a relationship strong—harmony or disagreement?

_____ 8. She can't sit still long enough to read a book; he loves to spend hours in a hammock playing his guitar.

_____ 9. No one has ever seen these two argue; they always seem to have the same opinions.

_____ 10. Should couples think about how similar or dissimilar their personalities are before committing themselves to marriage?

_____ 11. While he is at his best early in the morning, she thrives on staying up very late and sleeping in.

Answers begin on page 74.

Exercise 41 PARAGRAPHING II

In an essay, a new paragraph begins each time a new idea is developed or a new set of examples or details is presented. The first paragraph is an introduction that briefly states the topic and the main points to be made about the topic. The middle paragraphs are the body. Each paragraph in the body explains one of the main points to be made about the topic. The last paragraph is the conclusion. It summarizes the topic and the main points.

DIRECTIONS: The passage that follows is written without paragraph divisions. The passage should be divided into four paragraphs. Read the passage, and then answer the questions that follow it.

---

¹Language constantly changes. ²New words and new meanings for existing words are forever coming into popular usage. ³Some new words are short-lived as part of a society's vocabulary. ⁴Other newly coined words will withstand the test of time and remain as part of both informal usage and the standardized language found in the dictionary. ⁵Many new words that enter our daily vocabulary have their origins in science or technology. ⁶For example, from computer terminology we now have the words *software, program,* and *terminal.* ⁷Certainly, the words *program* and *terminal* were in the dictionary long before computers were even dreamed of; now, however, a new meaning has been added to each of these words. ⁸Many other words are adopted into the English language from other languages. ⁹*Macho* is a Spanish word that is now commonly used in English. ¹⁰No other single English word can convey so precisely the attitude of someone we call a "macho man." ¹¹*Croissant,* the French word for a type of flaky pastry, has become a standard item on American menus. ¹²A certain fast-food restaurant even offers "croissanwiches," sandwiches made with croissants. ¹³Perhaps one day *croissanwich* will make it into the dictionary; only time will tell. ¹⁴The above examples of words newly added to our vocabulary should give credence to the idea that language is living and growing. ¹⁵Our language changes to grow with us and to reflect our interests and ideas.

1. With what sentence should paragraph 2 begin? _____
2. With what sentence should paragraph 3 begin? _____
3. With what sentence should paragraph 4 begin? _____
4. Which sentences serve as the conclusion to the passage? _____
5. Which sentences give more information about the point made in sentence 5? _____

Answers begin on page 74.

Exercise 42   REVIEW OF PARAGRAPHING AND LOGIC

DIRECTIONS: Read each passage before answering the questions based on it. For each question, select the one best answer. Fill in the number in the answer grid that corresponds to the number of the best answer.

Questions 1–4

[1]People are often interested in the stories of presidents who died while serving their terms as leaders of the country. [2]Our assassinated presidents, most notably Lincoln and Kennedy, are often discussed and compared. [3]Franklin Roosevelt's death is readily recalled by those who were old enough in 1945 to mourn the loss of the great leader. [4]But two other presidents who died in office—William Henry Harrison and Zachary Taylor—are less well known. [5]William Henry Harrison, the ninth president of the United States, was distinctive in two ways. [6]First, he was the first U.S. president to die in office. [7]He served the shortest term of any president. [8]Harrison's death was not a dramatic one. [9]In fact, Harrison caught a serious cold while delivering his two-hour inaugural address in the freezing rain. [10]Harrison's cold developed into pneumonia, and he died just thirty-one days after being inaugurated. [11]Zachary Taylor also died a less than dramatic death. [12]Taylor is said to have gorged himself on cherries and cold milk after a Fourth of July celebration in the blazing sun. [13]He developed stomach cramps and died in the White House five days later.

1. Which sentence states the main idea of the passage?
   (1) sentence 1
   (2) sentence 2
   (3) sentence 4
   (4) sentence 9
   (5) sentence 13

2. If this passage were divided into three paragraphs, paragraph 3 would begin with
   (1) sentence 9.
   (2) sentence 10.
   (3) sentence 11.
   (4) sentence 12.
   (5) sentence 13.

3. Sentence 7 should
   (1) be left as is.
   (2) be omitted.
   (3) be attached to sentence 6 by office, but he.
   (4) begin with Nevertheless, he.
   (5) begin with Second, he.

(continued)

4. If an additional paragraph were added after sentence 13, it should

    (1) describe the assassinations of Kennedy and Lincoln.

    (2) give more details about Harrison's death.

    (3) give more details about Taylor's death.

    (4) summarize the similarities between the two little-known presidential deaths.

    (5) introduce James Garfield, another assassinated president.

4. ○ ○ ○ ○ ○
    1   2   3   4   5

Questions 5–8

[1]The state of New York has been actively pursuing a campaign to end underage drinking. [2]Last year, a new law was passed making it illegal for anyone under twenty-one to purchase alcoholic beverages. [3]Previously, only the sellers of alcohol to those under twenty-one were subject to legal action. [4]Consequently, the state recently implemented an under-twenty-one driver's license program. [5]It will take four full years to phase in the program. [6]For this reason, bartenders and store clerks must continue to check birthdates on the licenses of people who look young. [7]Under this program, all new licenses issued to young drivers will print in red the words *under twenty-one years of age* alongside the driver's photograph.

5. In sentence 4, *Consequently* should

    (1) remain.

    (2) be changed to *In addition.*

    (3) be changed to *Nevertheless.*

    (4) be changed to *In fact.*

    (5) be changed to *However.*

5. ○ ○ ○ ○ ○
    1   2   3   4   5

6. In sentence 6, the words *For this reason* should

    (1) remain.

    (2) be changed to *Furthermore.*

    (3) be changed to *However.*

    (4) be changed to *On the other hand.*

    (5) be changed to *Similarly.*

6. ○ ○ ○ ○ ○
    1   2   3   4   5

7. Sentence 7 should

    (1) remain where it is.

    (2) follow sentence 2.

    (3) follow sentence 3.

    (4) follow sentence 4.

    (5) be omitted.

7. ○ ○ ○ ○ ○
    1   2   3   4   5

8. If the passage were divided into two paragraphs, paragraph 2 would begin with

    (1) sentence 2.

    (2) sentence 3.

    (3) sentence 4.

    (4) sentence 5.

    (5) sentence 6.

8. ○ ○ ○ ○ ○
    1   2   3   4   5

Answers begin on page 74.

FINAL SKILLS INVENTORY

> **DIRECTIONS:** Beneath each sentence, you will find five ways to write the underlined part of the sentence. Answer (1) is always the same as the underlined part and may be the correct answer. Choose the correct answer, and fill in the number of that answer in the grid to the right.

Part I SENTENCE STRUCTURE, STYLE, DICTION

1. The apartment needed to be <u>cleaned, several coats of paint, and new carpeting</u> before the new tenants could move in.
   - **(1)** cleaned, several coats of paint, and new carpeting
   - **(2)** clean, several coats of paint, and new carpeting
   - **(3)** cleaned, painted, and new carpeting
   - **(4)** cleaned, painted, and carpeted
   - **(5)** given a good cleaning, several coats of paint, and carpeted

   1. ○ ○ ○ ○ ○
      1 2 3 4 5

2. <u>While I was using the copy machine in the library.</u>
   - **(1)** While I was using the copy machine in the library.
   - **(2)** It having been stolen while using the copy machine in the library.
   - **(3)** In the library, as I was using the copy machine.
   - **(4)** While I was using the copy machine in the library, my wallet was stolen.
   - **(5)** Using the copy machine, while my wallet was stolen in the library.

   2. ○ ○ ○ ○ ○
      1 2 3 4 5

3. Grace <u>couldn't hardly live</u> on the salary she earned at her full-time job.
   - **(1)** couldn't hardly live
   - **(2)** could not hardly live
   - **(3)** could hardly live
   - **(4)** hardly couldn't live
   - **(5)** could hardly not live

   3. ○ ○ ○ ○ ○
      1 2 3 4 5

4. <u>Today, in this present-day time period</u>, many children are being raised in single-parent homes.
   - **(1)** Today, in this present-day time period
   - **(2)** In today's present-day times
   - **(3)** Presently, in today's times
   - **(4)** In today's times
   - **(5)** Today,

   4. ○ ○ ○ ○ ○
      1 2 3 4 5

5. The new bride loved to look at <u>the ring on her finger with its shiny gold</u>.
   - **(1)** the ring on her finger with its shiny gold
   - **(2)** the shiny gold ring on her finger
   - **(3)** her finger, with its shiny gold on the ring
   - **(4)** the shiny gold on her finger in the ring
   - **(5)** the ring on her finger, with its shiny gold surface

   5. ○ ○ ○ ○ ○
      1 2 3 4 5

(continued)

64

6. Inez is learning word processing, it should help her find a higher-paying job.
   (1) word processing, it should
   (2) word processing it should
   (3) word processing and it should
   (4) word processing; it should
   (5) word processing; and it should

6. ○ ○ ○ ○ ○
   1 2 3 4 5

7. Although the second doctor confirmed the diagnosis, Mr. McGee's family refused to believe it.
   (1) diagnosis, Mr. McGee's family
   (2) diagnosis; Mr. McGee's family
   (3) diagnosis: Mr. McGee's family
   (4) diagnosis. Mr. McGee's family
   (5) diagnosis—Mr. McGee's family

7. ○ ○ ○ ○ ○
   1 2 3 4 5

8. Yesterday, the pitching coach tried out the new players; later today, he gave the other pitchers a workout.
   (1) gave
   (2) will give
   (3) has given
   (4) had given
   (5) gives

8. ○ ○ ○ ○ ○
   1 2 3 4 5

9. The fan cannot be run at the same time as the television unless the circuit will be overloaded.
   (1) unless
   (2) despite the fact that
   (3) because
   (4) after
   (5) so

9. ○ ○ ○ ○ ○
   1 2 3 4 5

10. The report stated that Sid had been removed from the firefighter training program because of his tendency to freak out in emergencies.
    (1) freak out
    (2) totally lose it
    (3) go crazy
    (4) manifest severe phobias
    (5) panic

10. ○ ○ ○ ○ ○
    1 2 3 4 5

11. When we saw the limb of the tree leaning against the house, we wondered if it had been hit by lightning.
    (1) it
    (2) that
    (3) the limb
    (4) anything
    (5) this

11. ○ ○ ○ ○ ○
    1 2 3 4 5

12. The burglar entered as quietly as a cat, but barked when he touched the live wire.
    (1) barked
    (2) yowled
    (3) grunted
    (4) brayed
    (5) squeaked

12. ○ ○ ○ ○ ○
    1 2 3 4 5

(continued)

13. Before the open heart surgery, Thelma must lose 20 pounds; overweight people are <u>poor surgical risks</u>.
    - (1) poor surgical risks
    - (2) risky in surgery
    - (3) risky surgically
    - (4) too risky for the surgeon
    - (5) a surgeon's nightmare

13. ○ ○ ○ ○ ○
    1 2 3 4 5

14. The deadline for voter registration is Tuesday; <u>moreover,</u> if you are ill or out of the country, you may have a week's extension.
    - (1) moreover
    - (2) therefore
    - (3) thus
    - (4) however
    - (5) as a result

14. ○ ○ ○ ○ ○
    1 2 3 4 5

15. We thought that the movie would be <u>good, and it</u> was awful.
    - (1) good, and it
    - (2) good; moreover, it
    - (3) good. Fortunately, it
    - (4) good, but it
    - (5) good, so it

15. ○ ○ ○ ○ ○
    1 2 3 4 5

16. <u>I read a book about the war that was long and tedious.</u>
    - (1) I read a book about the war that was long and tedious.
    - (2) I read a long and tedious book about the war.
    - (3) I read a book about the war that was said to be long and tedious.
    - (4) I read a book about the war; long and tedious as it was.
    - (5) I read a book about the war; it was long and tedious.

16. ○ ○ ○ ○ ○
    1 2 3 4 5

17. Jay Leno walked onto <u>the stage, and the audience cheered</u> loudly.
    - (1) the stage, and the audience cheered
    - (2) the stage and the audience cheered
    - (3) the stage; however, the audience cheered
    - (4) the stage, but the audience cheered
    - (5) the stage but the audience cheered

17. ○ ○ ○ ○ ○
    1 2 3 4 5

18. As soon as the plane had taken off, the pilot announced that poor weather conditions <u>are expected</u> throughout the flight.
    - (1) are expected
    - (2) have been expected
    - (3) were expected
    - (4) will be expected
    - (5) are being expected

18. ○ ○ ○ ○ ○
    1 2 3 4 5

19. I am looking forward to a <u>restful, entertaining, and one that is fun</u> vacation.
    - (1) restful, entertaining, and one that is fun
    - (2) restful, entertainment, and fun
    - (3) resting, entertaining, and one that is fun
    - (4) restful, entertaining, and fun
    - (5) rest, entertainment, and one that is fun

19. ○ ○ ○ ○ ○
    1 2 3 4 5

20. <u>In the playpen, the mother smiled at her child.</u>
    - (1) In the playpen, the mother smiled at her child.
    - (2) The mother smiled in the playpen at her child.
    - (3) The mother in the playpen smiled at her child.
    - (4) The mother, in the playpen, smiled at her child.
    - (5) The mother smiled at her child in the playpen.

20. ○ ○ ○ ○ ○
    1 2 3 4 5

(continued)

Part II ORGANIZATION AND LOGIC

> **DIRECTIONS:** Read each of the following passages, and answer the
> questions below. For each question, select the best
> answer, and fill in the answer grid to the right.

¹It is widely believed that the United States welcomes immigrants of all
nationalities. ²The United States is seen as a country with arms open to all.
³However, a study of U.S. immigration laws replaces the myth of "a country
of open arms" with the reality of a fairly restrictive immigration policy. ⁴As
early as 1798, the Alien Act authorized the president to deport aliens. ⁵The
Act of 1882 excluded "all lunatics and idiots" from immigration while also
excluding Chinese. ⁶The Act of 1891 excluded persons with certain specified
diseases and those who had been convicted of certain crimes. ⁷It is easy to
see why no one wanted sick people and criminals entering the country.
⁸Restrictions on immigration continued to be practiced in the twentieth
century. ⁹The Acts of 1907 and 1908 excluded persons "harmful" to labor
conditions in the U.S., specifically "Japanese and Korean laborers." ¹⁰The Act
of 1921 established quotas for specific immigrant groups, allowing mostly
northern or western Europeans to enter the country. ¹¹Asians were further
restricted entry by the Act of 1917. ¹²Furthermore, it is clear that U.S.
immigration policy has not always lived up to its open-armed policy.

21. Which sentence in the passage best states the topic of the passage?
    (1) sentence 1
    (2) sentence 2
    (3) sentence 3
    (4) sentence 8
    (5) sentence 12

22. Sentence 7 would be improved if
    (1) the sentence were omitted entirely.
    (2) the sentence were added to sentence 6 with the word because.
    (3) the sentence were changed to It is obvious that no one wanted
        sick people and criminals entering the country.
    (4) the sentence were placed before sentence 6.
    (5) the sentence were changed to This makes sense.

23. If the passage were to be divided into two paragraphs, the second
    paragraph would begin with
    (1) sentence 3.
    (2) sentence 5.
    (3) sentence 8.
    (4) sentence 9.
    (5) sentence 10.

24. Sentence 11 should be
    (1) omitted entirely.
    (2) placed after sentence 8.
    (3) placed after sentence 12.
    (4) placed after sentence 9.
    (5) left where it is.

25. The word Furthermore in sentence 12 should be
    (1) omitted entirely.
    (2) changed to In fact.
    (3) changed to In conclusion.
    (4) changed to However.
    (5) left as it is.

(continued)

¹The method of studying for a test depends on the type of test that is going to be taken. ²A test taker who wants to be wise about taking a test should find out what kinds of questions will be on each test given in the class. ³Knowledge of them will allow a test-wise student to study efficiently. ⁴For short-answer, fill-in-the-blank, and true-false tests, the test taker should learn as many specific facts and details as possible. ⁵For essay or oral tests, the student should learn about several general topics. ⁶Should be able to support these general topics with specific facts. ⁷For multiple-choice tests, it is often necessary to see relationships between facts and ideas rather than to recall the actual information. ⁸Therefore, the study approach for multiple-choice tests should focus on seeing relationships rather than on cramming for facts and details. ⁹All of these examples show that different types of test questions require different study approaches.

26. In sentence 2, <u>A test taker who wants to be wise about taking a test</u> should be
    (1) changed to <u>A test taker.</u>
    (2) changed to <u>Any test taker who wants to be wise about taking a test.</u>
    (3) changed to <u>Anyone who wants to be wise about taking a test.</u>
    (4) changed to <u>A wise test taker.</u>
    (5) left as is.

26. ○ ○ ○ ○ ○
    1 2 3 4 5

27. In sentence 3, <u>them</u> should be
    (1) changed to <u>these.</u>
    (2) changed to <u>possible question types.</u>
    (3) changed to <u>it.</u>
    (4) changed to <u>such.</u>
    (5) left as it is.

27. ○ ○ ○ ○ ○
    1 2 3 4 5

28. Sentence 6 should
    (1) be omitted.
    (2) begin with <u>The student.</u>
    (3) be joined to sentence 5 with the word <u>and.</u>
    (4) be joined to sentence 5 with a comma.
    (5) be left as it is.

28. ○ ○ ○ ○ ○
    1 2 3 4 5

29. Which sentence could be the topic sentence of the paragraph?
    (1) sentence 1
    (2) sentence 2
    (3) sentence 3
    (4) sentence 4
    (5) sentence 8

29. ○ ○ ○ ○ ○
    1 2 3 4 5

30. In sentence 8, <u>Therefore</u> should be
    (1) omitted.
    (2) changed to <u>On the other hand.</u>
    (3) changed to <u>Likewise.</u>
    (4) changed to <u>Nevertheless.</u>
    (5) left as it is.

30. ○ ○ ○ ○ ○
    1 2 3 4 5

Answers and Explanations begin on page 69.

FINAL SKILLS INVENTORY EVALUATION CHART

> **DIRECTIONS:** After completing the Final Skills Inventory, check your answers by using the Final Skills Inventory Answers and Explanations, pages 69 and 70. Write the total number of *correct* answers for each skill area on the blank lines below. If you have *more than one incorrect* answer in any skill area, you may need extra practice. The chart shows you which workbook exercises you'll need to review.

Skill Area	Item Numbers	Total	Number Correct	Exercise Numbers
Part I				
Correct sentence structure	2, 6, 7	3	_____	1–12, 26
Misplaced and dangling modifiers	5, 16, 20	3	_____	20–21, 26
Conjunctions	9, 14, 15	3	_____	2–4
Parallel structure	1, 19	2	_____	13–14, 17–18, 26
Verb tense	8, 18	2	_____	15–18, 26
Pronoun reference	11	1	_____	19
Style and diction	10	1	_____	22–23, 25
Redundancy	4	1	_____	24–25, 26
Double negatives	3	1	_____	24–25
Mixed comparisons	12	1	_____	24–25
Part II				
Topic sentences	21, 29	2	_____	27–28, 30
Unity	22	1	_____	29–30
Transitions	25	1	_____	31–32, 35
Logical order	24	1	_____	34–35
Conciseness and clarity	26, 27, 28	3	_____	33, 36–39
Paragraphing	23	1	_____	41–42

Note: Items 13, 17, and 30 are correct.

Answers and Explanations   FINAL SKILLS INVENTORY

> **DIRECTIONS:** After completing the Finals Skills Inventory (pages 63–67), use the Answers and Explanations to check your work. *On these pages*, circle the number of each item you correctly answered. Then turn to the Final Skills Inventory Evaluation Chart (page 68), and follow the directions given.

Part I SENTENCE STRUCTURE, STYLE, DICTION

1. **(4)** The three verbs in the correct version are all in the same form; in other words, the three verbs give the sentence parallel structure.

2. **(4)** The original sentence is a fragment, as are sentences (2), (3), and (5). Choice (4) is a complete sentence. It contains an independent clause—a subject and a predicate that express a complete thought.

3. **(3)** Only sentence (3) avoids the double negative of *not* and *hardly*.

4. **(5)** Only sentence (5) avoids the repetition of the idea of *present-day* and *today*. All the other choices are redundant.

5. **(2)** Only sentence (2) has the modifier *shiny gold* near the word *ring*, which it describes. In all the other choices, the modifier is misplaced.

6. **(4)** The original sentence is a run-on sentence. Version (4) correctly joins two closely related independent clauses into a compound sentence with a semicolon.

7. **(1)** Version (1) is correctly punctuated, with a comma following the introductory dependent clause.

8. **(2)** The words *later today* indicate that this action will happen in the future. Therefore, *will give* is the verb form that should be used.

9. **(3)** The correct subordinating conjunction for this sentence is *because*, which expresses the cause-effect relationship between the two clauses.

10. **(5)** Only the word *panic* is appropriate to the style of a sentence that discusses a report. The other choices are either slang expressions or unnecessarily formal.

11. **(3)** The pronoun reference is unclear in the original sentence; does *it* refer to the tree or to the house? To clarify the sentence's meaning, the pronoun *it* must be replaced by the noun *limb*.

12. **(2)** The verb *yowled* fits with the comparison of the burglar to a cat. *Barked* is characteristic of a dog and creates a mixed comparison.

13. **(1)** Choice (1) is clear and concise.

14. **(4)** The relationship between the two ideas in the sentence is best expressed by the word *however*.

(continued)

15. (4) The correct conjunction is *but.*

16. (2) The word *that* is unclear—was the book or the war long and tedious? Only choice (2) clarifies the meaning of the sentence.

17. (1) The conjunction *and* preceded by a comma correctly joins the two independent clauses.

18. (3) Since the pilot made his announcement after the plane had taken off, the simple past form, *were expected*, is appropriate.

19. (4) This is the only choice that uses the parallel structure of three adjectives to describe the vacation.

20. (5) Only in version (5) is the prepositional phrase *in the playpen* placed next to the word it describes (*child*).

Part II ORGANIZATION AND LOGIC

21. (3) Sentence (3) states the topic of the passage, which is that U.S. immigration policy has actually been restrictive rather than totally open.

22. (1) This sentence is irrelevant to the passage. The rest of the material gives details on specific policies and laws and does not deal with the rationale behind the policies.

23. (3) A second paragraph could begin with those acts passed in the twentieth century, separating them from those passed earlier.

24. (4) To keep the sentences in chronological (time) order, the sentence dealing with an act passed in 1917 should go before the sentence discussing the act passed in 1921.

25. (3) The transition should be *in conclusion.* Only this choice correctly introduces a summarizing sentence.

26. (4) This choice is the most concise—it states the full meaning of the thought in the fewest possible words.

27. (2) Choice (2) is the only one that clarifies the meaning of what will allow efficient study. All the other choices are vague or unclear.

28. (3) Sentence (6) is a fragment. With the addition of the word *and*, it can be joined to the preceding sentence.

29. (1) Sentence 1 best expresses the complete topic of the whole paragraph.

30. (5) The word *Therefore* shows the correct transition between the two sentences.

ANSWER KEY

EXERCISE 1

1. <u>Margarita</u> <u>sings</u>
2. <u>brother and I</u> <u>fight</u>
3. <u>Go</u> (you)
4. <u>It</u> <u>is</u>
5. <u>you</u> <u>Are going</u>
6. <u>Help</u> (you)
7. <u>Sam</u> <u>has</u>
8. <u>Porsche</u> <u>was dented</u>
9. <u>we</u> <u>felt</u>
10. <u>New Orleans</u> <u>is</u>
11. <u>Ms. Jenks</u> <u>interviewed</u>
12. <u>Red beans and rice</u> <u>make</u>
13. <u>review</u> (you)
14. <u>Tania</u> <u>seems</u>
15. <u>I</u> <u>became</u>

EXERCISE 2

1. , and
2. , so
3. , but
4. , and
5. , but *or*, yet
6. , so
7. , and
8. , and
9. , or
10. , and

EXERCISE 3

1. ; moreover,
   ; furthermore,
   ; in addition,
2. ; therefore,
   ; as a result,
   ; consequently,
3. ; however,
4. ; moreover,
   ; furthermore,
   ; in addition,
5. ; moreover,
   ; furthermore;
   ; in addition,
6. ; otherwise,

EXERCISE 4

1. While you were at lunch,
2. when the weather is nice
3. If you have any questions,
4. before winter comes
5. because it was boring
6. Although Carm likes living in the U.S.,
7. until he was thirty

EXERCISE 5

1. simple
2. complex
3. compound
4. complex
5. compound
6. simple
7. simple
8. complex
9. compound
10. compound

EXERCISE 6

1. S
2. F
3. F
4. S
5. S
6. F
7. S
8. S
9. S
10. S
11. S
12. F
13. S
14. S
15. S
16. F
17. S
18. S
19. F
20. S

EXERCISE 7

Although vegetables are nutritious, I have hated them ever since I was a child. The very sight of cauliflower makes me break into a cold sweat. Smothering it with cheese sauce doesn't help **because I can still taste the cauliflower.** Broccoli also makes me sick. I hate the way it smells while it is cooking. I dislike beets even more. Steamed, boiled, baked, or broiled, they look bad and taste worse. Spinach is the worst of all. **Whenever I lay eyes on it**, I think of lawn cuttings. To me, fruits, dairy products, and meats are delicious. But when it comes to vegetables, count me out.

EXERCISE 8

1. b
2. b
3. b
4. a
5. a
6. b
7. a
8. b
9. b
10. a
11. b
12. a

EXERCISE 9

1. 1
2. 5
3. 2
4. 1
5. 3
6. 1
7. 3
8. 1

EXERCISE 10

1.	RO	9.	RO
2.	C	10.	RO
3.	C	11.	RO
4.	RO	12.	C
5.	C	13.	RO
6.	RO	14.	C
7.	C	15.	RO
8.	RO		

EXERCISE 11

1.	c	4.	c
2.	a	5.	b
3.	c		

EXERCISE 12

1.	3	6.	4
2.	1	7.	1
3.	3	8.	3
4.	5	9.	4
5.	2	10.	5

EXERCISE 13

1.	b	5.	a
2.	b	6.	b
3.	a	7.	b
4.	b		

EXERCISE 14

1. save, spend
2. her good sense of humor, her intelligence
3. be content, have faith
4. cutting, touching
5. a flash attachment
6. getting to know you
7. Writing
8. swimming
9. more convincingly

EXERCISE 15

1. came
2. needs *or* will need
3. skip *or* have skipped
4. cooked
5. got
6. had forgotten
7. left *or* were leaving
8. had
9. began
10. has seemed

EXERCISE 16

1. liked
2. had read *or* read
3. OK
4. expect *or* are expecting
5. knew
6. missed
7. was falling *or* fell
8. have felt
9. had
10. will ask
11. played *or* were playing
12. should call
13. threw
14. OK

EXERCISE 17

1.	4	11.	2
2.	2	12.	3
3.	1	13.	3
4.	5	14.	4
5.	3	15.	2
6.	3	16.	4
7.	4	17.	4
8.	4	18.	1
9.	5	19.	4
10.	3	20.	3

EXERCISE 18

1.	2	7.	4
2.	4	8.	1
3.	1	9.	3
4.	3	10.	5
5.	5	11.	4
6.	2		

EXERCISE 19

1.	2	5.	5
2.	4	6.	2
3.	3	7.	5
4.	2		

EXERCISE 20

1.	4	6.	1
2.	2	7.	5
3.	1	8.	3
4.	3	9.	4
5.	2	10.	3

EXERCISE 21

Various answers are possible.
Here are some suggestions:
1. While I was watching the rain, time got away from me.
2. The snacks, which are on the kitchen counter, are for the guests.
3. Whistling and singing, the campers filled the road.
4. The baby, who needed a dry diaper, cried for his mother.
5. Barb's husband, who had worked until 8 P.M., walked the dog.
6. The salesman showed the customer a watch that kept perfect time.
7. The lost child, who had tears in her tiny eyes, was comforted by the police officer.
8. I enjoy steaming hot herb tea with lemon.

EXERCISE 22

1. unbearable
2. assertive and confident
3. place
4. males
5. On family outings
6. funniest guy
7. model
8. a tattletale
9. the most effectively
10. argue

EXERCISE 23

1. petite
2. bloomed
3. butcher
4. pawed over
5. racket
6. brutality
7. alcoholics

EXERCISE 24

Various answers are possible.
Here are some suggestions.
1. I was late because the bus broke down.
2. Like glowing embers, her black eyes sparkled with gold.
3. The office was a hive of activity, with all the workers buzzing around.
4. Today, Americans need to believe in the rights and responsibilities of citizenship.
5. I don't have any money for tickets.
6. The international students need help filling out their papers.

EXERCISE 25

1. 4
2. 2
3. 1
4. 2
5. 4
6. 2
7. 5
8. 3

EXERCISE 26

1. 3
2. 4
3. 2
4. 1
5. 5
6. 4
7. 2
8. 4
9. 3
10. 4
11. 2
12. 3

EXERCISE 27

1. c
2. b
3. e
4. d

EXERCISE 28

1. a
2. c
3. d

EXERCISE 29

1. 3
2. 5
3. 4
4. 3
5. 4
6. 2
7. 4
8. 1
9. 5
10. 3

EXERCISE 30

Topic Sentences	Irrelevant Sentences
1. 1	4
2. 5	none
3. 1	5
4. 1	4, 5
5. 1	3, 6
6. 1	4, 7
7. 3	4, 6
8. 6	3
9. 1	3

EXERCISE 31

1. c
2. a
3. c
4. b
5. c
6. d

74

EXERCISE 32

1. In addition
2. Therefore
3. Eventually
4. First
5. At the same time
6. Then
7. Finally
8. For example
9. Moreover
10. Consequently

EXERCISE 33

1. repeating sentence structure
2. repeating key words
3. using pronouns

EXERCISE 34

1. 3, 4, 2, 1, 5	**4.** 2, 1, 4, 5, 3
2. 3, 4, 1, 2, 5	**5.** 1, 5, 2, 3, 4
3. 1, 3, 2, 4, 5	

EXERCISE 35

1. 4	**5.** 4
2. 2	**6.** 4
3. 5	**7.** 1
4. 1	**8.** 4

EXERCISE 36

1. 2	**4.** 5
2. 3	
3. 5	

EXERCISE 37

Various answers are possible. Here is one suggestion:

Ever since talk-show host Oprah Winfrey lost nearly 70 pounds, thousands of Americans have decided to try the liquid-formula diet plan that she used. Experts now believe, however, that liquid diets often contribute to physical or psychological problems for people on liquid diets. Apparently, many of these dieters develop intense cravings for foods containing high percentages of fat and calories. Furthermore, they become accustomed to living without real food, and they fear that they will lose all control when they begin eating again.

EXERCISE 38

1. 3	**6.** 1
2. 3	**7.** 4
3. 2	**8.** 3
4. 4	**9.** 2
5. 2	**10.** 2

EXERCISE 39

1. 2	**7.** 2
2. 5	**8.** 3
3. 4	**9.** 4
4. 1	**10.** 3
5. 3	**11.** 5
6. 5	

EXERCISE 40

1. III
2. I
3. III
4. II
5. II
6. III
7. I
8. III
9. II
10. I
11. III

EXERCISE 41

1. 5
2. 8
3. 14
4. 14 and 15
5. 6 and 7

EXERCISE 42

1. 3	**5.** 2
2. 3	**6.** 1
3. 5	**7.** 4
4. 4	**8.** 3